QUICK TIPS FOR CATCHING HALIBUT

EASY-TO-LEARN INFORMATION FOR THE ANXIOUS ANGLER!

BY CHARLIE WHITE
Illustrated by
NELSON DEWEY

COPYRIGHT © 1997
CHARLIE WHITE
and
NELSON DEWEY
ALL RIGHTS RESERVED

Cover photo: Brandy Laidler, Charlie's stepdaughter, poses with the 121-pound halibut caught by Charlie, Greg Sampson, and Mike Fast, off D'arcy Island near Sidney, B.C.

Introduction

This is the first of a series of "Quick Tips" books designed for the person in a hurry; the man or woman who seldom reads the instructions on a new product. In our high speed world, they just want to get on with it.

YOU CAN SKIM QUICKLY THROUGH THE FIRST SECTION AND LEARN THE "BASICS" -- and when you want more details, you can read the main text!

My earlier "how-to" books were written for a complete cross-section of anglers, from beginner to expert, combining serious information with light-hearted cartoons by a master cartoonist, Nelson Dewey. Our purpose was to make it more fun to learn a recreational subject.

This book will use the same technique, but with less detail. We will give step-by-step instructions on the most popular and productive techniques, backed up with observations from our studies with our remotely controlled underwater television camera system.

The people in a hurry have probably already moved on, so let's join them and "get on with it".

All About Halibut

Halibut is the largest member of the flatfish family, closely related to flounder... they begin life more or less like a "normal" fish, swimming upright with one eye on each side of the head. When they are about five months old the left eye actually migrates across the head to the right side and the fish assume the familiar, flattened shape.

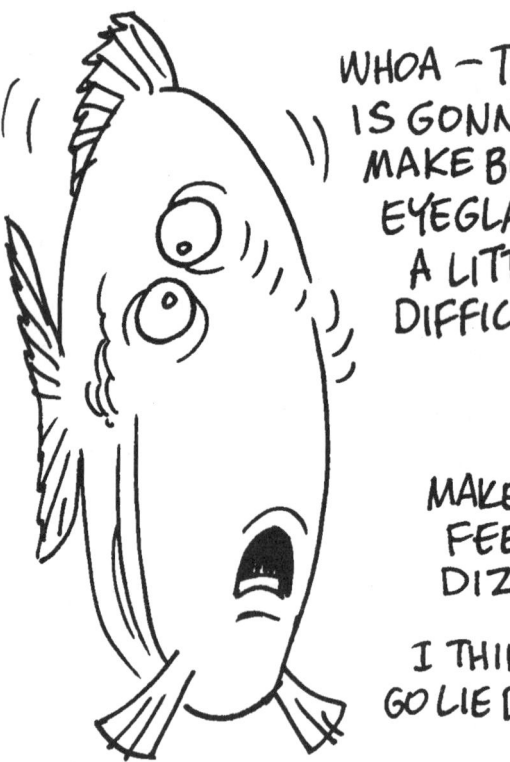

By the time they reach ten years of age, males average 20 pounds and females closer to 40 pounds. Halibut just keep on growing and growing!

We have all heard stories about the 200-pounders that can tow a boat for miles... my own experience with halibut suggests that most are much smaller.

Halibut concentrations increase as you move North. Best fishing is in British Columbia and Alaska

BEST DEPTHS -- BY SEASON AND AREA

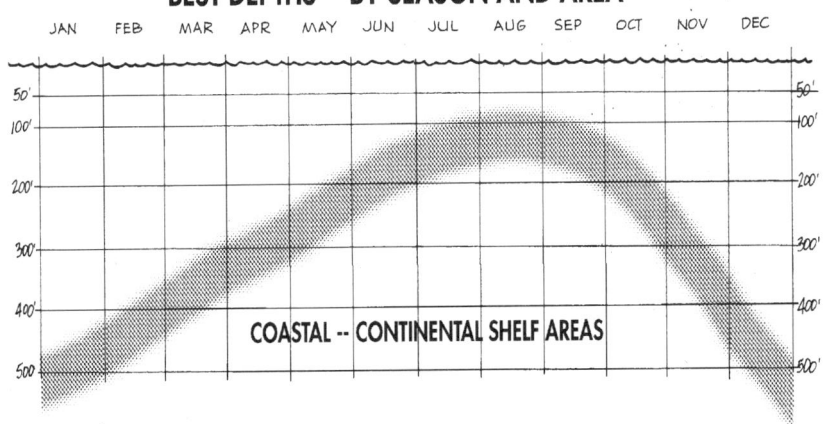

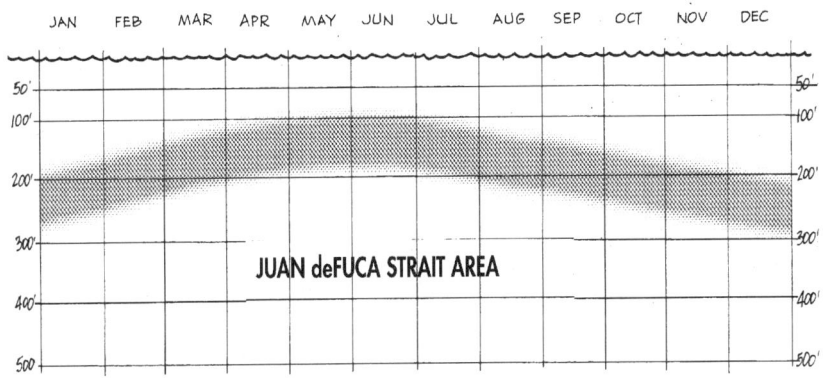

WHERE TO FIND HALIBUT

UNDERWATER HUMPS

WHERE TO FIND HALIBUT

SHELVES OR PLATEAUS

WHERE TO FIND HALIBUT

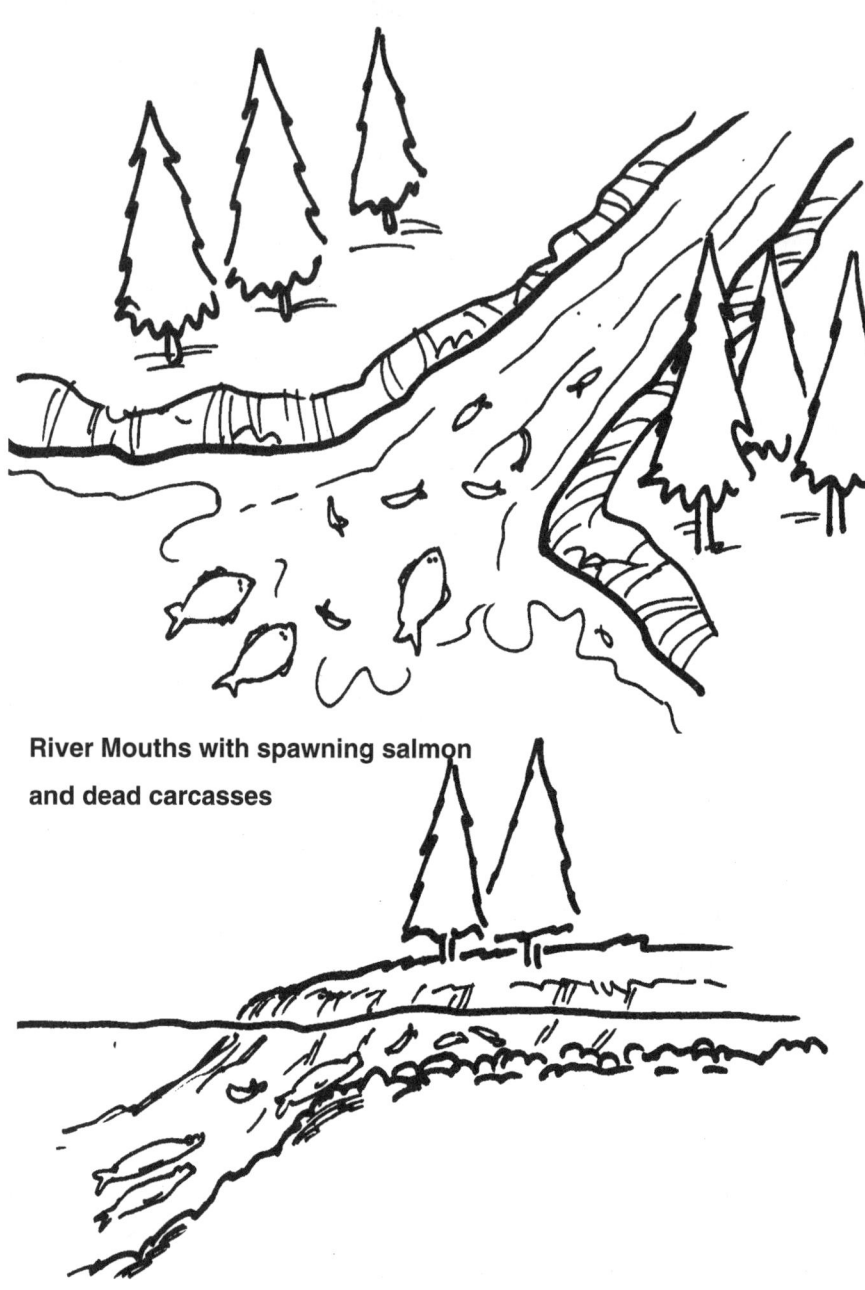

River Mouths with spawning salmon and dead carcasses

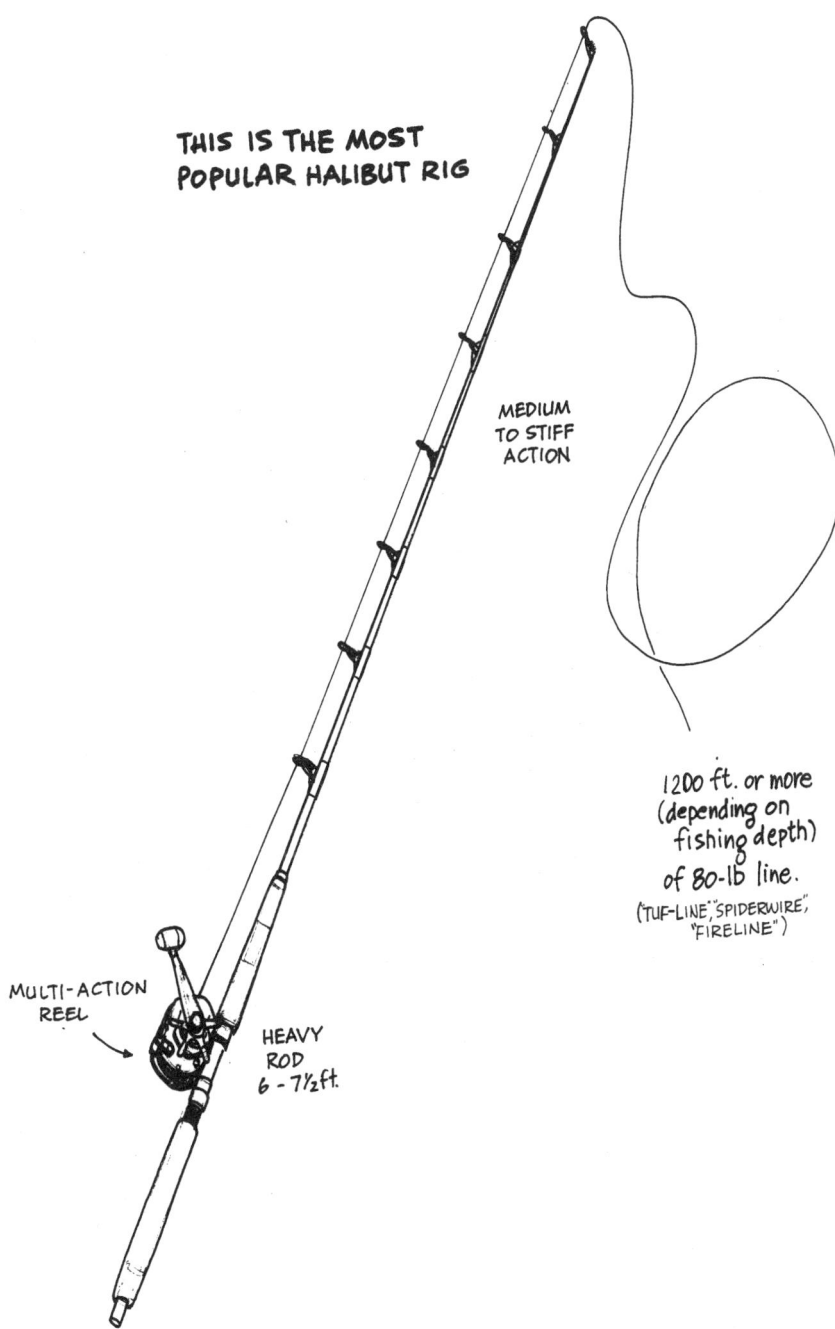

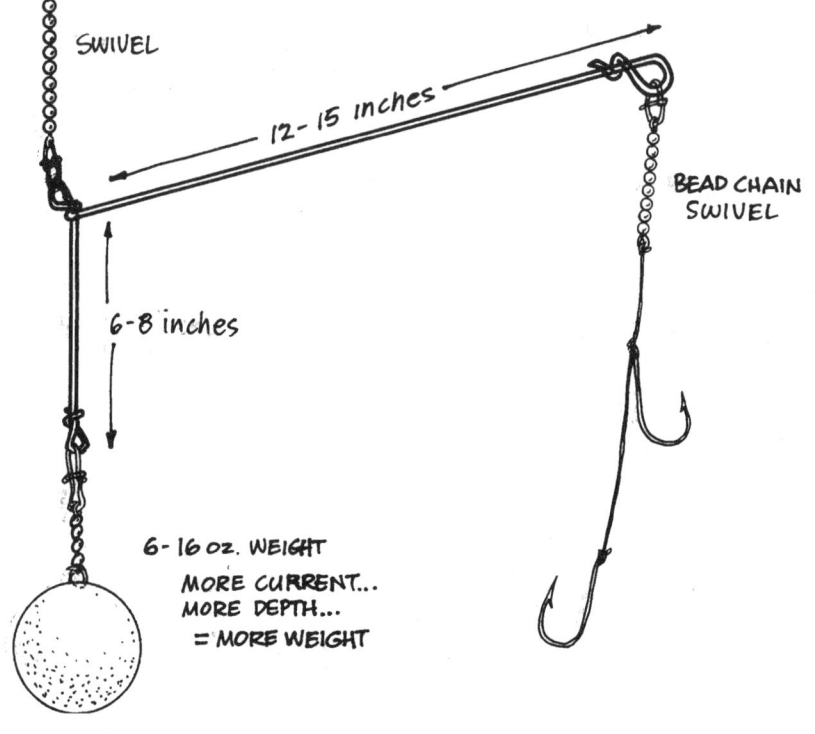

TWO-HOOK HERRING RIG

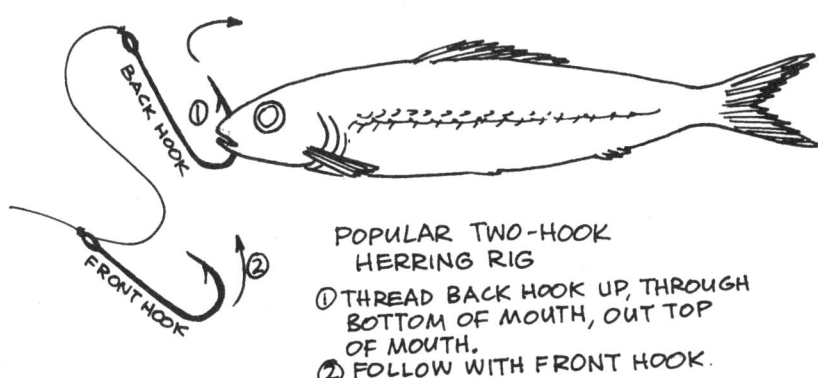

POPULAR TWO-HOOK HERRING RIG
① THREAD BACK HOOK UP, THROUGH BOTTOM OF MOUTH, OUT TOP OF MOUTH.
② FOLLOW WITH FRONT HOOK.

③ PUT BACK HOOK THROUGH TOP OF EYE SOCKET.
④ FOLLOW WITH FRONT HOOK.

⑥ INSERT FRONT HOOK IN OPPOSITE SIDE.

⑦ TAKE UP SLACK IN LEADER.

⑤ INSERT BACK HOOK IN SIDE NEAR TAIL.

ARTIFICIAL LURES

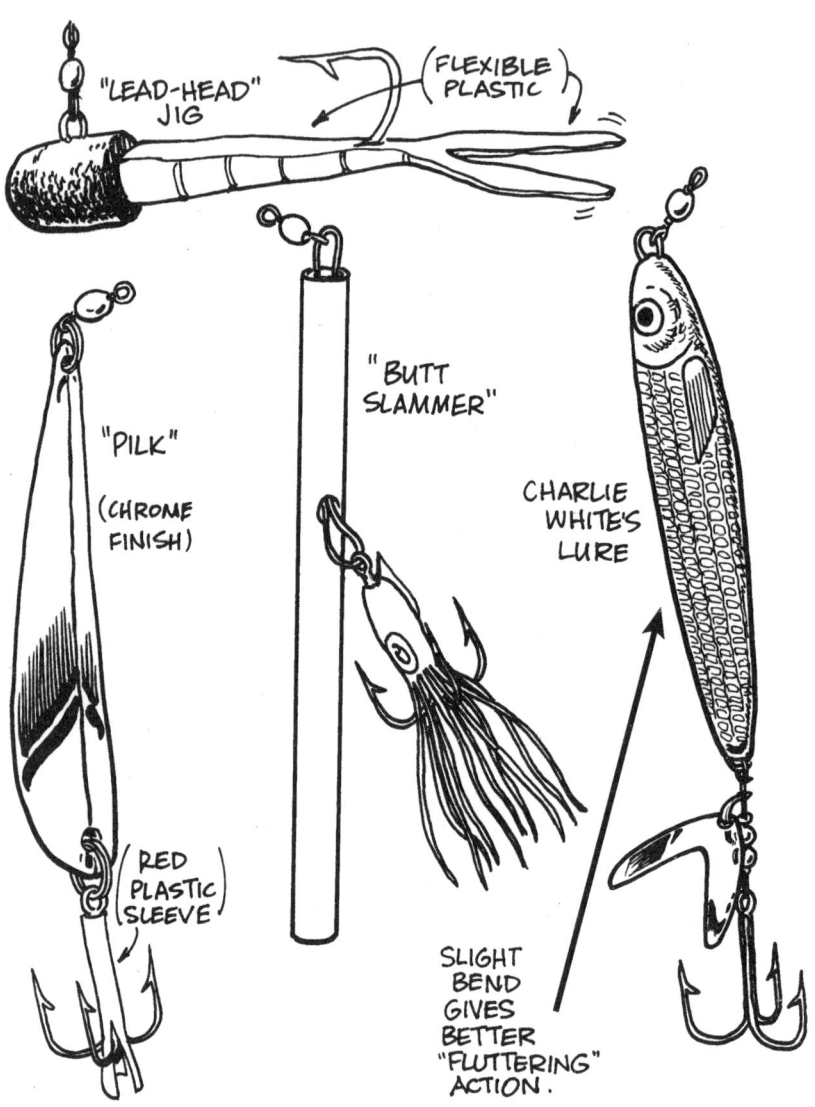

KEEP YOUR HOOKS "STICKY-SHARP"

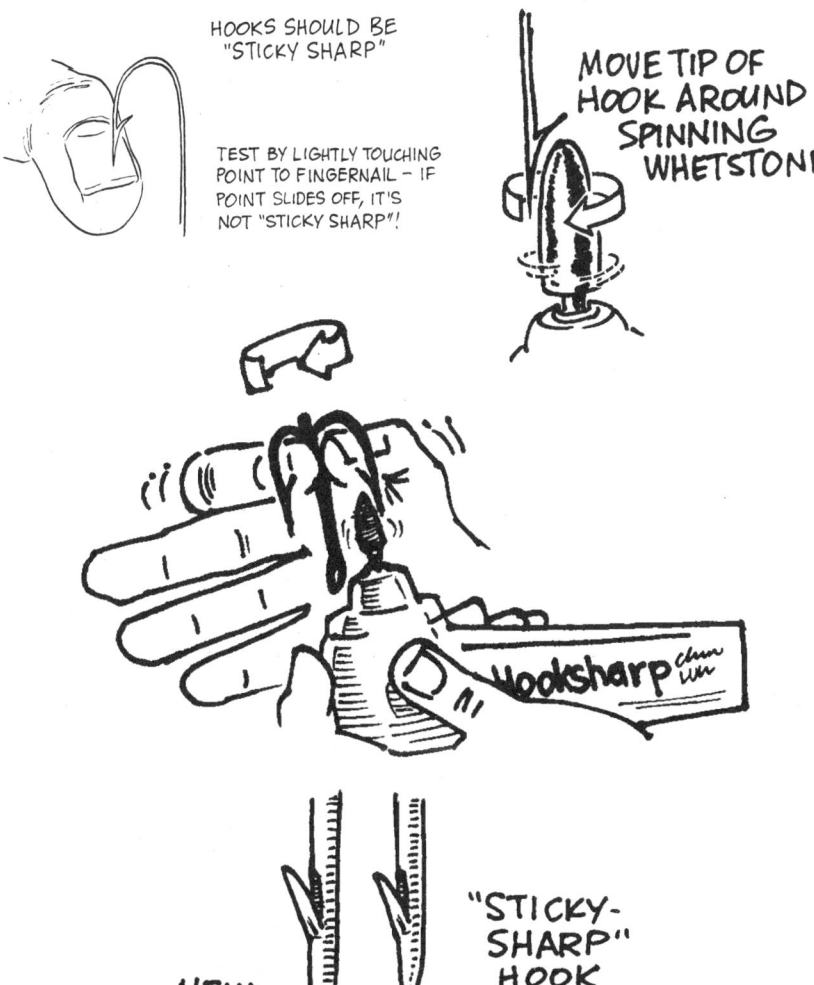

Combination -- Bait and Artificial Lures

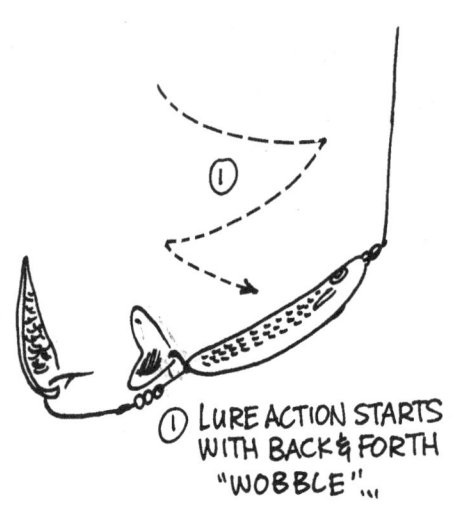

① LURE ACTION STARTS WITH BACK & FORTH "WOBBLE"...

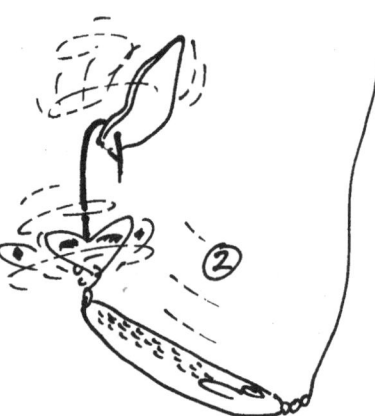

② THEN BAIT & SPINNER BEGIN TO "FLUTTER"

Jigging Technique -- Lift slowly, then drop.

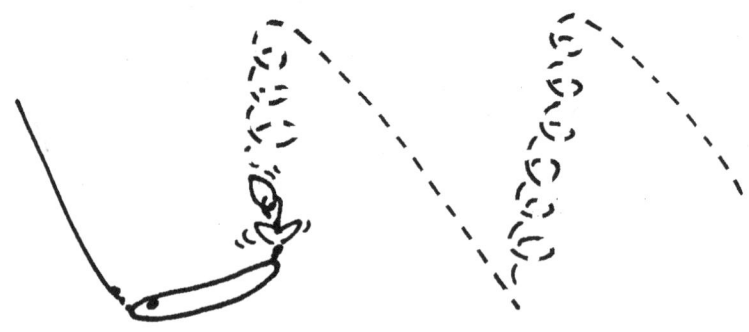

Jigging technique for bait

Lift rod tip slowly -- then drop it abruptly so weight thumps onto bottom. Pause (vary -- ten secondss - two minutes).

PAUSE   PAUSE

Jigging technique for artificial lure

Lift and drop rod tip -- as with bait -- but keep lure active. Pauses should be only 2 - 5 seconds.

GO FOR VERTICAL ANGLE

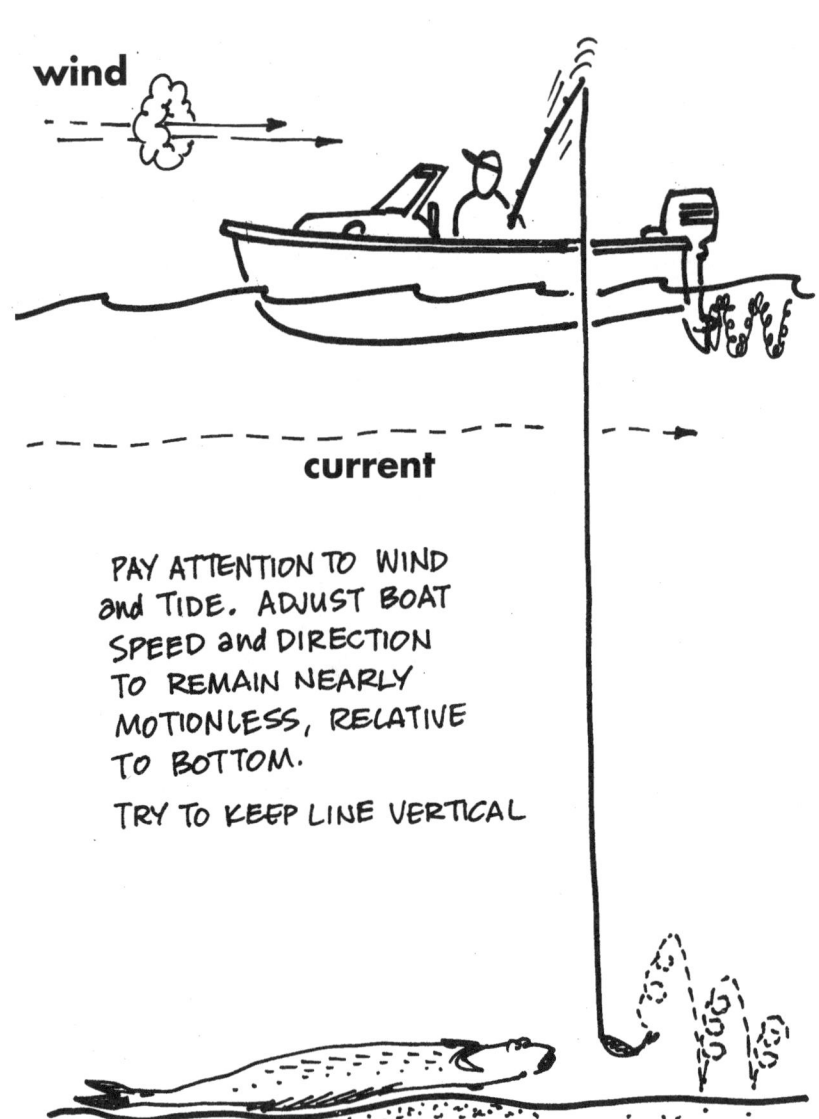

PLAYING HALIBUT

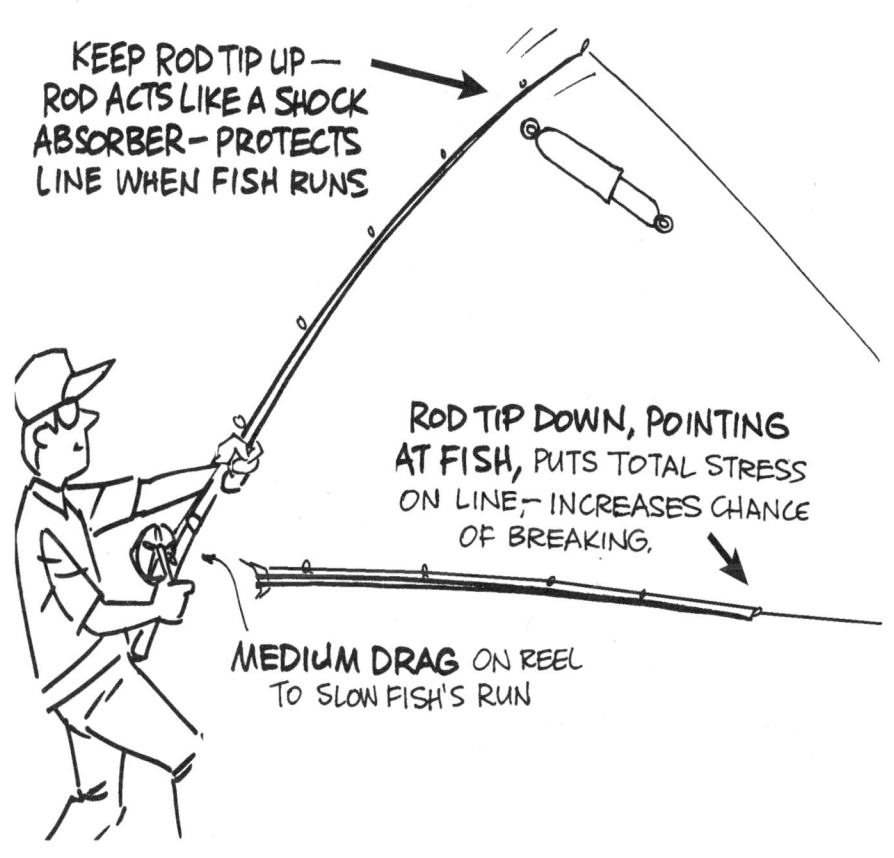

PLAYING HALIBUT

KEEP THE FISH MOVING AND AWAY FROM BOTTOM

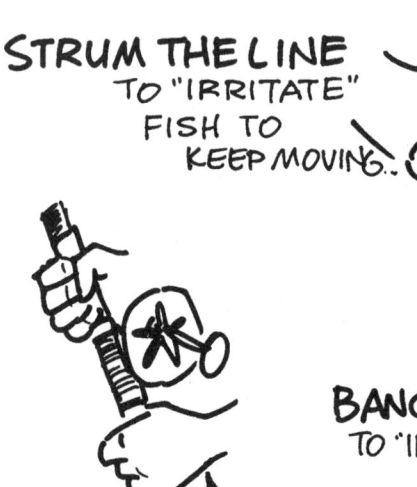

STRUM THE LINE TO "IRRITATE" FISH TO KEEP MOVING...

BANG ROD BUTT TO "IRRITATE" FISH...

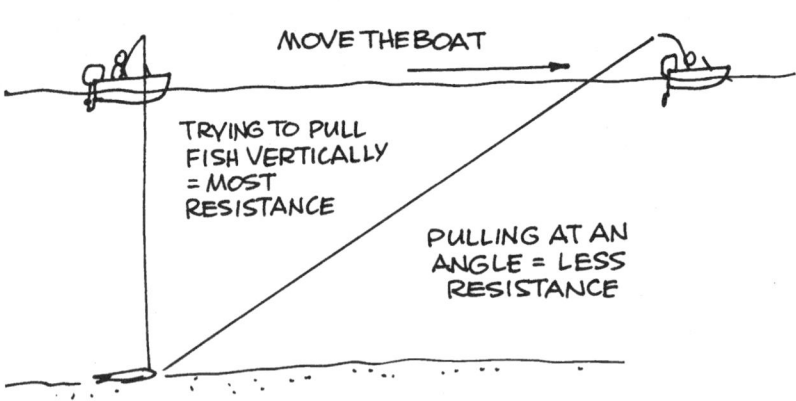

MOVE THE BOAT

TRYING TO PULL FISH VERTICALLY = MOST RESISTANCE

PULLING AT AN ANGLE = LESS RESISTANCE

LANDING HALIBUT

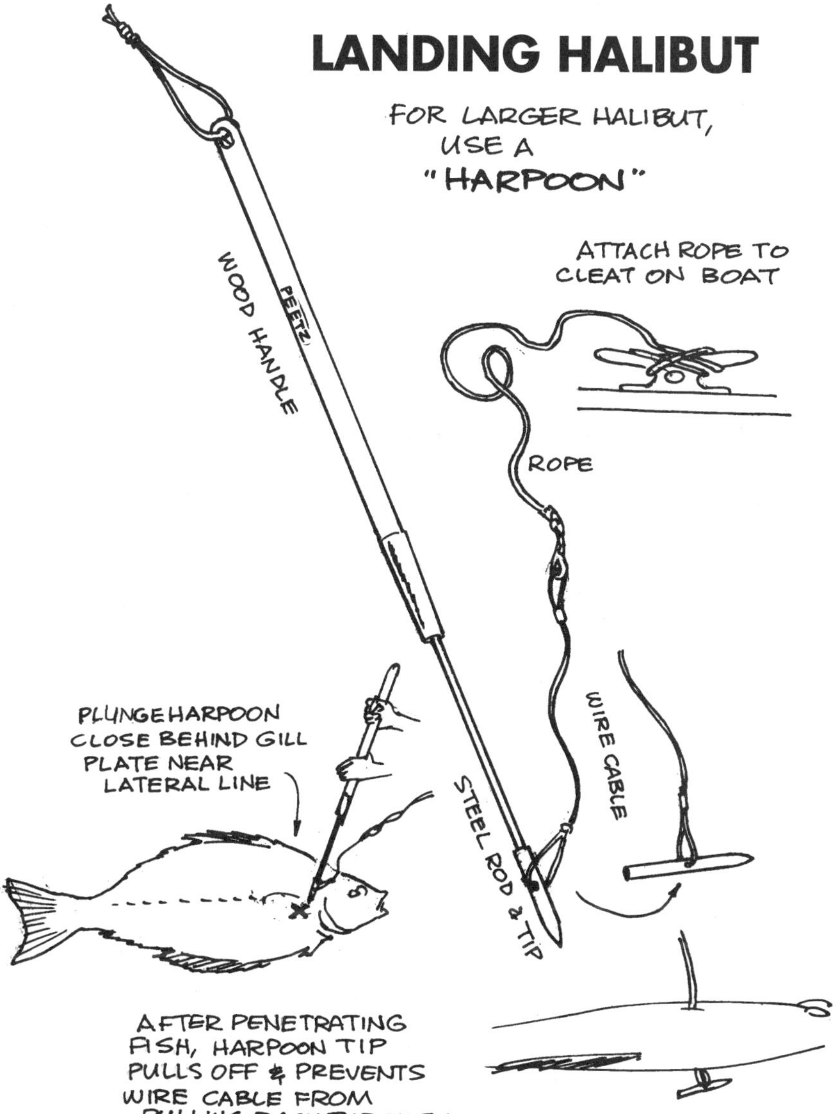

FOR LARGER HALIBUT, USE A "HARPOON"

WOOD HANDLE (PEETZ)

ATTACH ROPE TO CLEAT ON BOAT

ROPE

WIRE CABLE

STEEL ROD & TIP

PLUNGE HARPOON CLOSE BEHIND GILL PLATE NEAR LATERAL LINE

AFTER PENETRATING FISH, HARPOON TIP PULLS OFF & PREVENTS WIRE CABLE FROM PULLING BACK THROUGH

DON'T LIFT ITS HEAD

NET SMALLER HALIBUT HEAD-FIRST

IMPROVE YOUR CHANCES WITH SCENT

FISH RESPOND TO SMELL AS WELL AS SIGHT AND SOUND STIMULI.

AN ATTRACTANT (SUCH AS "X-10") CAN PROVIDE ADDED INCENTIVE FOR HALIBUT TO INVESTIGATE YOUR LURE!

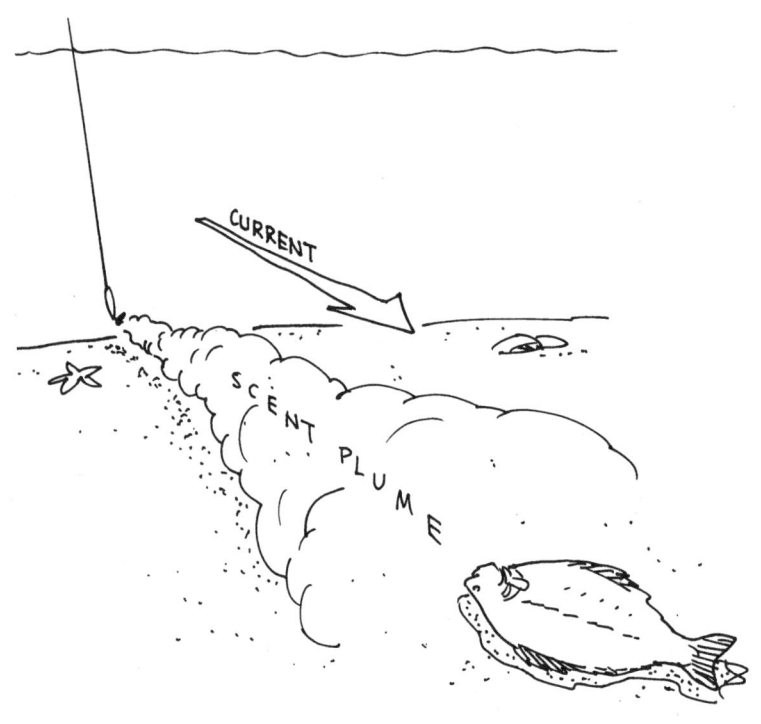

X-10 CAN BE EFFECTIVE AN HOUR OR MORE... BUT FOR BEST RESULTS, ADD A FEW DROPS EACH TIME YOU CHECK YOUR LURE OR BAIT.

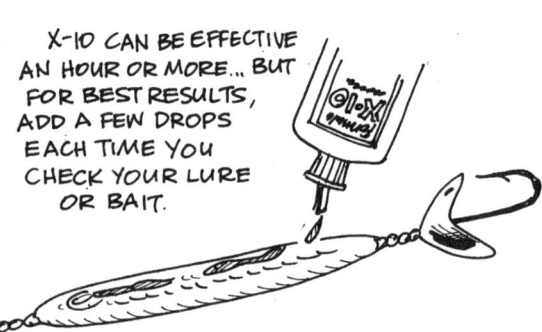

HOW HALIBUT STRIKE

HALIBUT SENSES LURE...

..."INHALES" LURE WITH TERRIFIC FORCE...

BAIT AND "X-10" ENTICES FISH TO HOLD LURE LONGER (AND INCREASE CHANCE OF BEING HOOKED) BEFORE SPITTING OUT.

CLEANING AND FILLETING

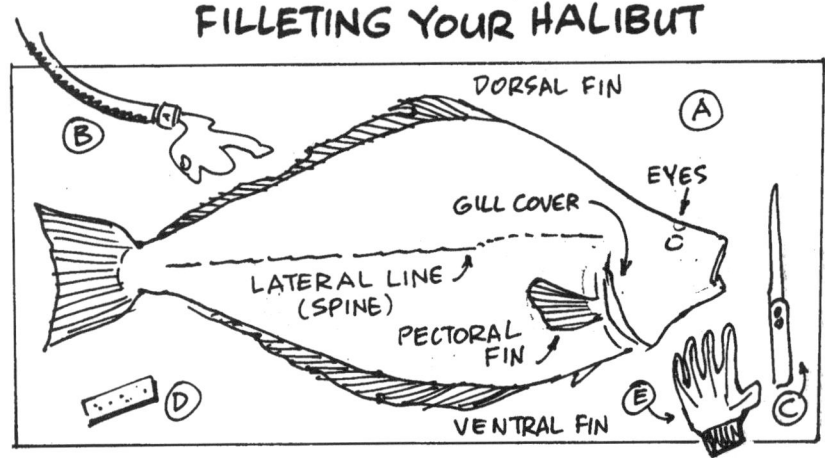

... IS IDEALLY DONE ON A WAIST-HIGH TABLE Ⓐ COVERED WITH BURLAP, INDOOR-OUTDOOR CARPET, ETC., TO KEEP FISH FROM SLIDING AROUND.

A WATER SOURCE WILL KEEP WORK AREA CLEAR OF BLOOD, ETC. Ⓑ

A GOOD QUALITY FILLETING KNIFE Ⓒ - 8" TO 12" BLADE - IS A NECESSITY... AS IS A STONE Ⓓ OR OTHER SHARPENING DEVICE. RE-SHARPEN THE KNIFE FREQUENTLY!

A HEAVY, COARSE GLOVE Ⓔ - FOR THE HAND NOT WIELDING THE KNIFE - HELPS HOLD SLIPPERY FISH - AND PROTECTS FROM SHARP SPINES, BONES...

CLEANING AND FILLETING

① WITH HALIBUT DARK-SIDE UP, START BY REMOVING "CHEEK" FLESH (BETWEEN EYES AND GILL COVER).

FEEL FOR SOFT AREA, INSERT KNIFE AT SHALLOW ANGLE.

Be sure to get the tasty "halibut Cheeks"!

② IF YOU DON'T CUT COMPLETELY AROUND THE CHEEK, YOU CAN USE THE RESULTING "HINGE" OF SKIN TO FOLD THE CHEEK OPEN...

③ ...AND SLICE THE MEAT FROM THE SKIN FLAP.

LEAVE SKIN FLAP(S) ATTACHED TO FISH.

(IF YOU PREFER, YOU CAN CUT ALL THE WAY AROUND THE CHEEK AND REMOVE IT COMPLETELY. FIND THE METHOD THAT WORKS FOR YOU!)

CLEANING AND FILLETING

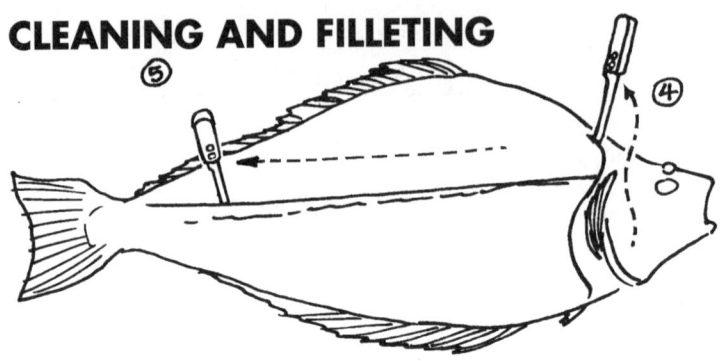

TURN FISH DARK SIDE UP.

④ MAKE A CURVED CUT BEHIND THE PECTORAL FIN, FROM THE VENTRAL FIN TO JUST AHEAD OF DORSAL FIN.

CUT CAREFULLY NEAR VENTRAL AREA TO AVOID OPENING THE STOMACH (MESSY!).

⑤ CUT DEEPLY (HOLD KNIFE NEAR-VERTICAL) ALONG LATERAL LINE, FROM CUT ④ BACK TO UPPER EDGE OF TAIL.

⑥ CUT UPPER FILLET BY LIFTING AT CENTER CUT (⑤) AND SLIDING KNIFE FLAT AGAINST BONES. CUT AND "PEEL" FILLET TOWARDS TAIL.

YOU CAN LEAVE ANOTHER "HINGE" AT THE TAIL (LIKE THE CHEEK ③) AND SLICE MEAT AWAY FROM THE SKIN... OR COMPLETELY REMOVE FILLET AND SLICE MEAT AWAY LATER.

CLEANING AND FILLETING

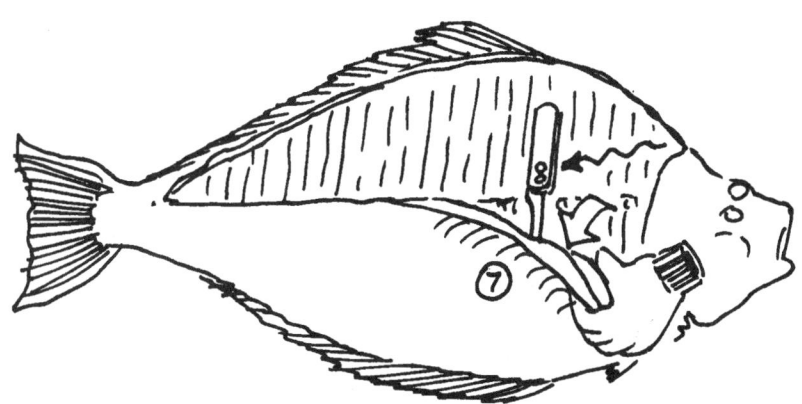

⑦ CUT AWAY LOWER FILLET – "PEEL" DOWN AND TOWARDS TAIL.

☆ USE CARE CUTTING NEAR STOMACH AREA ☆

⑧ TURN FISH OVER AND REPEAT ① THRU ⑦ ON LIGHT SIDE.

SECTION 2
HALIBUT FISHING --
"IN-DEPTH"

CONTENTS

JUST FOR THE HALIBUT..........30

HALIBUT GEOGRAPHY..........36

WHEN TO CATCH 'EM..........38

TACKLE -- PLAY 'EM OR WINCH 'EM.....42

FIND THE FEEDING LOCATIONS..........51

LURES & BAITS..........58

LURE PRESENTATION..........67

HOW HALIBUT BITE.......72

PLAYING & LANDING HALIBUT......74

CARE & CLEANING OF THE CATCH....84

GOURMET RECIPES.....86

Chapter One

"Just for the Halibut!"

Halibut is the largest member of the flatfish family, closely related to flounder, but also very similar to sole and sanddab. Their major claim to fame is their growth pattern, far outdistancing the sole and flounder which seldom exceed ten pounds in weight.

All flatfish begin life more or less like a "normal" fish, swimming upright with one eye on each side of the head. When they are about five months old and about 25 mm(1 inch) in length, a remarkable transition takes place. The left eye actually migrates across the head to the right side and the fish assume the familiar, flattened shape.

All flatfish, including halibut, grow rather slowly, seldom exceeding a foot in length by the age of three years. They feed primarily on small crabs, shrimp and fish. Many flatfish are nearing maturity at this age, but the halibut, especially the females, are just getting started on their growth curve.

By the time they reach ten years of age, males average 20 pounds and females closer to 40 pounds. This is still quite slow growth when compared to other North Pacific gamefish. Chinook Salmon average 17 to 20 pounds at four years of age with some specimens exceeding 60 or even 70 pounds, at less than half the age of a comparably sized halibut.

Since all Pacific Salmon spawn and die by four or five years of age (except for rare specimens who postpone spawning to age six or even seven), their faster growth rate can't win the contest for absolute size. Halibut just keep on growing and growing!

We have all heard stories about the 200-pounders that can tow a boat for miles, and seen pictures of hanging specimens that towered above their captor. Many fishing lodges in British Columbia and Alaska report numbers of halibut over 100 pounds each season, and a few lucky anglers get the thrill of a lifetime in battling a 200-pounder.

My own experience with halibut suggests that most are much smaller. Watching the daily weigh-in at fishing lodges in British Columbia and Alaska, the great majority of halibut are about the size of a prime Chinook Salmon, 20 to 30 pounds in weight. A few reach 40 or 50 pounds and even fewer move the scales toward the century mark.

My personal biggest was a 121-pound giant caught just east of Sidney, B.C. in about 130 feet of water. We got an 85-pounder in the same spot about ten days later. Both fish were taken while bottom bouncing a nine- inch herring.

I've also taken several halibut while trolling for salmon. One was a 50 pounder who struck when I was trolling herring in Barkley Sound near Harrison Cove Lodge. (This catch was recorded on video by 12-time Grammy winning composer, David Foster, who wrote the theme music for my television series, "Charlie White's Fishing Machine").

Another was taken while trolling on a sandy bottom at Sidney Spit near my home, while testing my new Picture Perfect Lure, which uses a color photo image of a herring to trigger strikes of salmon and other gamefish.

We tried off and on for ten years to get underwater pictures of halibut behavior with our remotely controlled underwater television research cameras, but halibut are usually found in conditions unsuitable for our work.

We tried Juan de Fuca Strait on the U.S.-Canada border; Barkley Sound, Clayoquot Sound and Nootka Sound on the West Coast of Vancouver Island; Shearwater, Bella-Bella, and Hakai Pass on the central Coast; Dawson Harbour and Naden Harbour in the Queen Charlottes; and Work Channel, Edye Pass and Fort Simpson in the Prince Rupert area.

Three problems plagued us continually. Most halibut hot spots are in 180 to 300 feet of water, far too deep for our cameras. Water was often murky, and open ocean swells exposed the camera to banging hard on the bottom as our research boat came down in the trough between waves.

We finally had a stroke of good luck (persistence pays off — eventually) when we visited Farewell Harbour Yacht Club in Johnstone Strait near the north end of Vancouver Island. Flat calm water, with good clarity, combined with bright sun, allowed us to see the bottom in 55 to 60 feet.

We watched, for the first time ever witnessed by man, a huge halibut approach our metal jig with a piece of herring attached. Unfortunately, we had been pestered by cabezons and rockfish in our first drifts across the harbor bottom, and we had deliberately dulled the hooks so we could shake them off without bringing in the camera rig to reset after each hook-up. Now that the hooks had been blunted, our first halibut appeared!

He (or more likely she, since the big ones are all female) circled the jig twice, then sucked it in while we watched in awe. The lure flew back out of her mouth in a split second,

as soon as she touched the metal jig. The lure was covered with our Formula X-10 fish feeding stimulant, so she came back twice more, inhaling the dull hooks and blowing them back out again, while we watched helplessly.

We got another chance the next day, when a 65 pound fish sucked in the bait right on camera, then took off in a reel screaming run. (This entire adventure is available on video, complete with slow motion replays. See details in the back of the book.)

In the summer of 1996, we took our research crew and camera to

Whaler's Cove Lodge near Angoon in Southeast Alaska. We fished Chatham Strait, looking for halibut in shallow water. In five memorable days, we recorded over 15 on-camera halibut strikes, some in water as shallow as 40 feet, with good water clarity.

On one occasion, we counted five halibut on-camera at once. These underwater observations -- with subsequent analysis on our slow motion broadcast quality playback units -- gave us fresh insights into halibut feeding behavior which we will discuss in this book.

Chapter Two

"The Geography of Halibut"

Halibut is a cold water fish. Salmon are the classic cold water fish, preferring temperatures of 50° to 53° Fahrenheit (10° to 12° Celsius), but halibut like it colder still, from a few degrees above freezing to 41° or 42° (from 2° to 9° Celsius). This, in large degree, determines their geographical distribution.

Southern Boundary

On the Pacific Coast, there is a major temperature break at Point Conception near Santa Barbara, California. Swimming beaches south of this area support summer temperatures as much as 10° to 20° warmer than those north toward San Francisco.

Point Conception is also the location of a major faunal break. Marine species change radically in this area, with tropical fishes (including tuna and marlin) found to the south, and salmon, halibut and other temperate and cold water species to the north. (The area between Santa Barbara and San Francisco is also home to increasing numbers of "Jaws"

himself, the Great White Shark; they migrate south to give birth, then move back north to feed on the increasing populations of the environmentally protected seals and sea lions.)

There are halibut south of Point Conception, but this is a different animal. The California halibut is found from northern California to well south of the Mexican border. Most fish are ten pounds or less, but there are enough 20 pounders to keep things interesting. Trophy specimens reach 35 to 40 pounds, with record fish just over 50 pounds.

"CALIFORNIA HALIBUT"

Northern Range

Halibut populations increase as we move north from California, through Oregon and Washington, to the excellent halibut fishing available in British Columbia and Alaska. Halibut are found in abundance in all Alaska off-shore waters right across the Aleutian Chain past Dutch Harbor. Halibut are also found off the coast of Russia and down the coast to the island of Hokkaido in Japan.

Chapter Three

"When to Catch Them"

Halibut can be caught 12 months of the year if the season is open and you have the boat and equipment to get to them.

In addition to being a cold water fish, halibut tend to be a deep water fish. Most lodges in British Columbia and Alaska report that most halibut hot spots are from 150 to 250 or 300 feet deep, and this is in the late spring or summer months when they are usually most shallow.

During the winter months, from late October until March, the

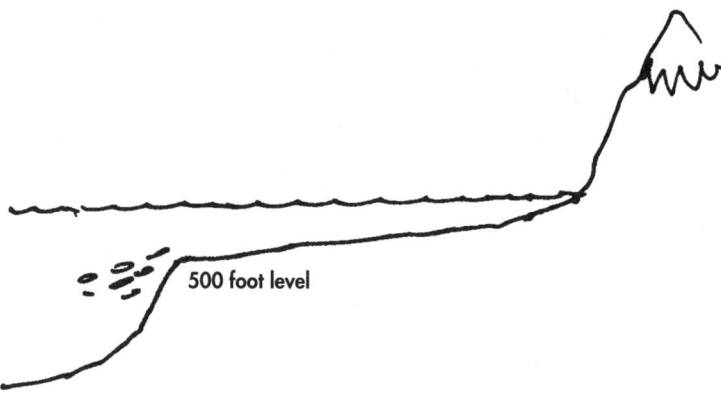

larger halibut spawn along the edge of the continental shelf at depths over 500 feet and, for all practical purposes, are not available for the sports angler.

"Smaller" halibut, up to 40 or 50 pounds can be taken in Juan de Fuca Strait throughout the winter months, often by anglers trolling deep along the bottom for winter chinook salmon. Those targeting on halibut usually jig in 150 to 200 feet, but halibut are taken as shallow as 75 feet or as deep as 300 feet with very heavy jigs, or bait with a 12 to 16 ounce sinker.

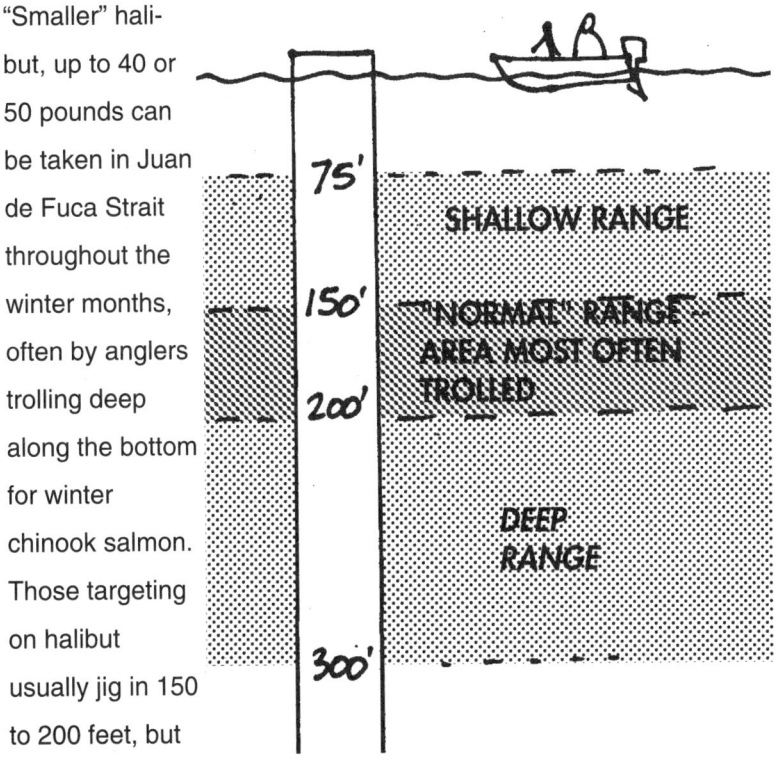

In March and April, the big halibut begin to move inshore off Washington, Oregon and Southern British Columbia. This is the time of year I fish for halibut off D'Arcy Island about five miles southeast of Sidney, B.C., and ten miles northeast of Victoria. We bottom bounce big herring and drift with the tide over a sandy bottom about 130 feet below the surface.

This is where we boated the 121 pound and 85 pound fish mentioned earlier. Both were hooked within 20 minutes of low slack tide, my favorite time to fish for halibut.

The fishing here seems to taper off as the season progresses, with little success (or little fishing effort) after mid-June.

In many areas off the west coast and adjacent to the open Pacific, good halibut fishing continues all summer and into mid-September. Most of the major port cities in Oregon - Coos Bay, Newport, Tillamook are jumping off places for halibut, as are Ilwaco, Westport, Neah Bay, and Sekiu along the Washington coast.

In British Columbia, halibut fishing is growing in popularity in such salmon hot spots as Barkley Sound, and throughout the Queen Charlottes and Prince Rupert areas.

The whole state of Alaska is a halibut hot spot all summer long, with the halibut moving into shallow water in July and August to forage on the spawning salmon as they enter their fresh water nursery streams. Cook Inlet is the major sport fishing area for halibut, but Kodiak Island, Seward and Homer are other popular locations off the Central Alaska Coast. In South east Alaska, the big catches are coming from the Yakutat area all the way to Ketchikan and the U.S. - Canada border.

We were very impressed with the Angoon area on Chatham Strait when we stayed at Whaler's Cove Lodge, and studied halibut behavior with our underwater research cameras. Every evening the fish cleaning station was stacked with halibut ranging from 20-pound "chicken" halibut to the over 100- pound "barn doors". The halibut are caught deep in late May and June, reach their shallowest point in mid to late August, then move deeper again in September - October.

Chapter Four

"Play Them or Winch Them - Halibut Tackle"

Your really never know (unless you have an underwater camera) just how big that next halibut will be until you are locked in battle. It could be a 15-pound "chicken" or a 150-pound "slab", so you need to plan your tackle accordingly.

I love light tackle and single action rods, so I tend to the more sporting gear, even though I would be hopelessly inadequate to handle anything over 100 pounds. In our television show on Farewell Harbour halibut, I played and landed a 65 pounder on 20-pound test line, a single action reel, and a medium flexible 6 foot rod.

Since most halibut are in the 20-to-40 pound range, you can have some great sport playing them on relatively light tackle. If meat is your primary consideration, you can go for heavier tackle, with a multiplying action slipping clutch reel, to take out some of the risk (and the fun) of landing a stubborn fish. If you hook a monster "barn door", you'll also be glad you opted for heavy tackle. If you are targeting trophy halibut, by location and technique, you should definitely go for the stronger tackle.

Light tackle is practical in shallow water conditions, where you don't need heavy sinkers to reach the bottom. If there is little wind or tide, a 6 to 8 ounce sinker will get your gear down to 100 feet or more. A strong tide or wind will require heavier weights or a downrigger to hold the gear on the bottom. If you use weights of a pound or more, you are losing much of the fun of light tackle fishing, and you might just as well use heavier gear.

Another disadvantage of light tackle is getting a solid hook up. A limber rod and nylon line (which can stretch up to 25% or more) makes it very difficult to sink a hook past the barb in the tough jaw of any halibut.

Rods

I use a stiffer, shorter rod (six feet) for light tackle halibut than I do for salmon, where I use an eight- to ten-foot rod with a stiff butt and very limber tip. I still prefer monofilament over the new technology lines (Spiderwire, Berkley Fireline) although they are much stronger and thinner, and stretch less than 5%. I'm going to give them a try next season.

There are three basic types of reels:

Single action - A simple spool of line which rotates around a central post. No multiplying action or slipping clutches. When the fish pulls, you let the reel spin or risk breaking the line or tearing loose the hook. These reels are less expensive and easier to maintain, with no gears or clutch mechanisms.

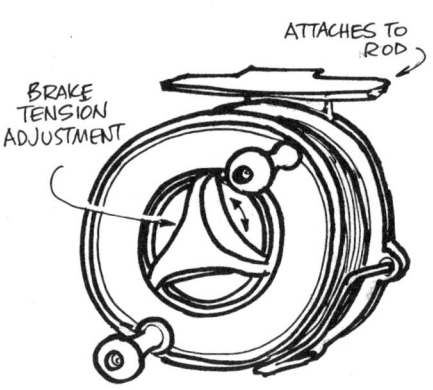

These reels are also more fun to use, in my opinion. You "feel" every twist and jerk of the fish, "palming" the reel to slow down a run, or winding fast to keep tension on a fish swimming toward the boat. Some popular brands are Daiwa, Shimano, Mitchell, Alvey, and Hardy.

Slip - Clutch, Multiplying Action - These can range from small bait casting reels to huge "cranks" used for marlin and other big tropical gamefish. They use gears to "multiply" the winding action at the handle. Every turn of the handle is converted to three or four turns of the reel spool. This allows the angler to bring in line very quickly when necessary to keep up with a fish rushing toward the boat.

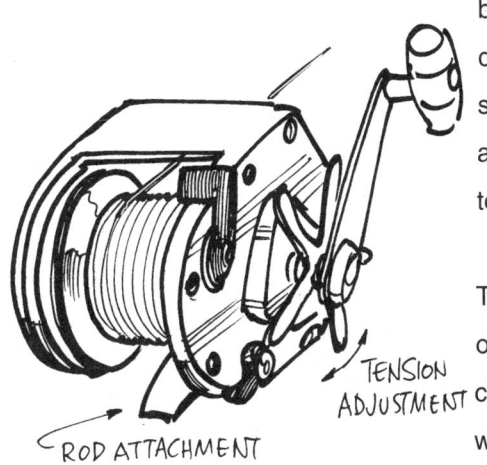

These reels also use one of a variety of clutch mechanisms which allow the reel to run out against the adjustable drag, while the reel handle remains stationary. This eliminates the problem of holding the reel too tight against a running fish, or letting it run too freely.

On the other side of the coin, these "safety" features take some of the "fun" and skill requirement out of playing any fish. With the clutch replacing the reel "palming" action, you get no "feel" of the fish, no opportunity to apply a variable tension to "guide" a fish, or to experience the excitement of winding like mad to keep the line from going slack.

For more fish in the boat, or when going for that once-in-a-lifetime trophy, put out the heavy tackle and winch them in!

Spinning reels - Used more for casting than for trolling or jigging. Not very practical for halibut, unless you want to try for

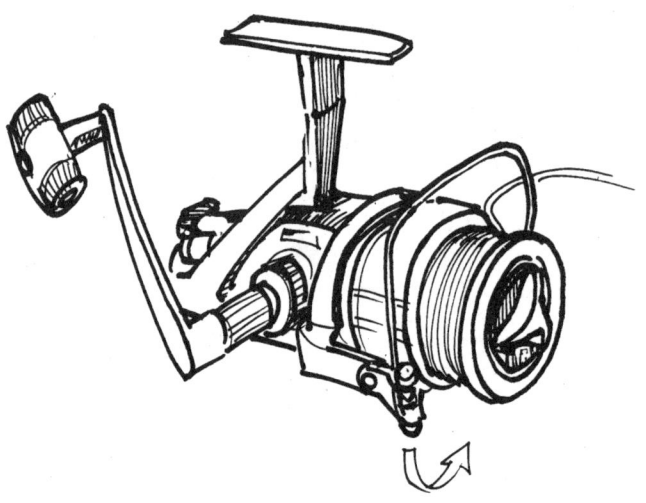

some ultra light tackle fun on small fish in shallow water. The same holds true for fly rods and reels.

Hooks - Many articles on halibut fishing are very specific on hook details. After watching them strike on my underwater camera, I'm not sure you can be that specific, since there are many types of strikes.

For bait fishing, I'm not sold on the popular circle hook. This hook, first used in the commercial long line fishery, was so effective that it is now the standard hook in the industry, used in over 95% of all set lines. Set lines are not monitored full time, so the fish has to hook itself, swallowing the hook, or twisting and turning until it catches in the jaw, or slips out completely.

From my observations, the effectiveness of a hook is directly proportional to the size and angle of the point of the hook in relation to the shank. I've never liked the "eagle claw" toe-in of many sport hooks. Dragging these hooks across your hand results in far less hook-ups than a straight point.

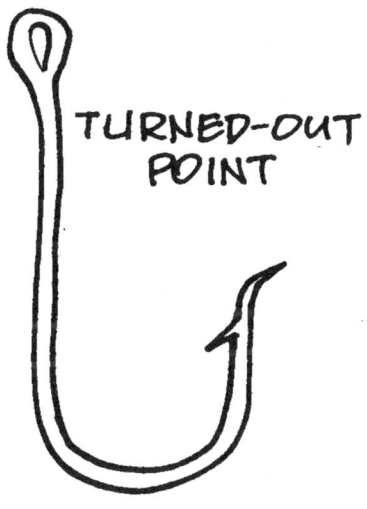

In tests using many hook styles dropped into a salmon head device, hooks with a toe-in caught in the jaw 43% of the time. Straightening the toe-in improved it to over 60%. I know one commercial troller who actually turns the hook points outward, and reports a much higher successful strike percentage.

Straight point hooks can be shaken loose by a thrashing fish on a slack line, but that is what fishing is all about. Maintaining a steady tension when playing the fish is the mark of a skillful fisher, and very few fish will be lost on a tight line.

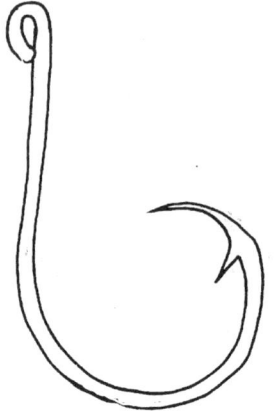

Circle hooks, as the name implies, turn the point right back close to the shank. Once this hook takes hold, it is extremely difficult to dislodge, which makes it ideal for unattended set lines or long lines, but this full 90° toe-in makes it a very low percentage hooker, in my opinion.

Hook size will vary depending on the size of the fish in the area and the method of fishing. A 5/0 single hook is large enough, especially if rigged in tandem on a big herring or salmon belly, but it should be a medium gauge thickness. When targeting trophy fish, size 8/0 to 12/0 heavy gauge hooks are most appropriate.

When fishing artificial jigs, you might want to consider treble hooks. In the hook set tests mentioned above, an off-set single with a straight point caught in the jaw 63% of the time, the

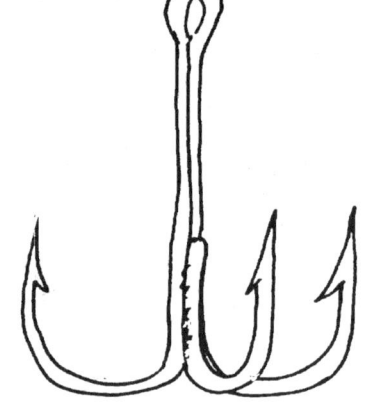

best for any single hook. Trebles, on the other hand, got successful hook-ups more than 85% of the time.

There is no question in my mind that a treble hook, with three sharp points protruding in three directions, offers the best chance for hooking any fish, but trebles do have their drawbacks:

1. After a fish is hooked, the opposing points of the treble can sometimes work against each other, sometimes leveraging the impaled hook right out of the fish's jaw.

2. The leader or line can jam in the tight crevice where the three hook shanks came together. This can result in reversing the angle of tension against the hook. The reversed hook is now being pulled right out of the mouth!

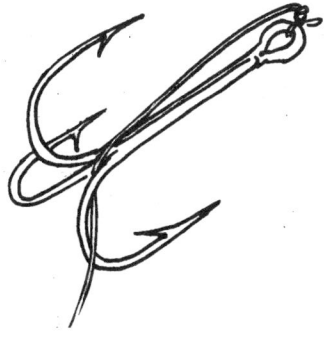

3. Trebles are much more likely to snag when jigged over a rocky or weedy bottom. The multiple angle protrusion of the hook points, so helpful in increasing hooking power, is now a major drawback. It's no fun losing expensive jigs on the bottom, or spending frus-

trating time trying to release a snagged lure.

A word of caution: If you are using one of the new technology lines(Spectra, Spiderwire, Gorilla, Fireline) be extremely careful when pulling on it, especially with bare hands. This thin, powerful line can slice into your flesh like a knife through hot butter. I find it better to move off to an angle opposite to the "snag angle", then wrap 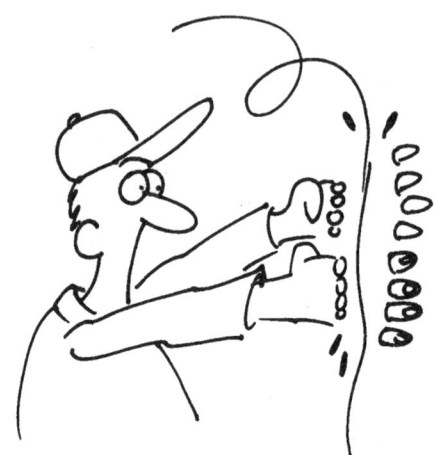 around a cleat and move slowly away until it pulls loose, or breaks the line.

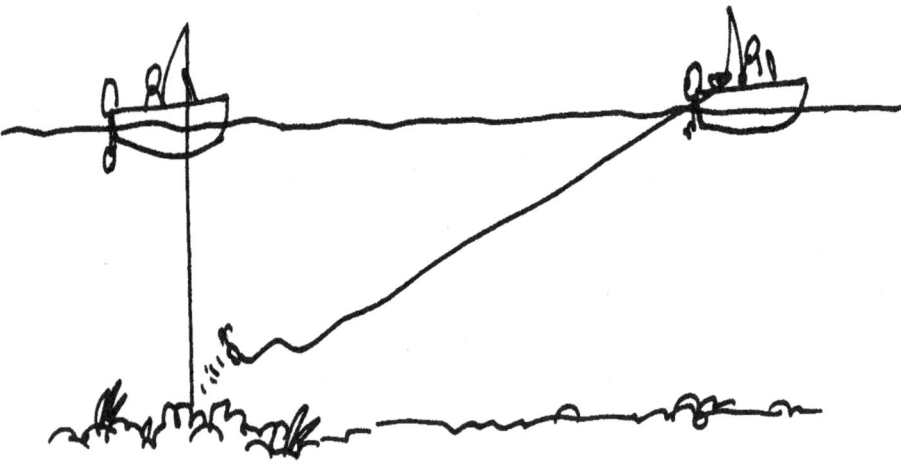

Chapter 5

"Finding the Feeding Locations"

There are a number of basic rules for finding salmon and other gamefish in saltwater, and some of them apply to halibut. There are also rules that don't apply, and some that are unique to halibut fishing.

1. **Humps or underwater hilltops** - These areas of "high ground" slightly (or sometimes substantially) above the surrounding terrain are often excellent places to look for feeding

UNDERWATER HUMPS

halibut. Hungry fish came up from the surrounding deep water to feed on the baitfish and groundfish which often gather near such bottom structures.

As the "bite" subsides and the tide picks up, I find it is often productive to drift onto the downstream side of the pinnacle to follow the fish down.

2. **Shelves or plateaus** - These flat or gently sloping areas, adjacent to deeper water, are often very productive. Just as they move onto humps, the halibut move up from deeper water to find food on these gently sloping areas.

SHELVES OR PLATEAUS

3. **River mouths where salmon congregate** - Halibut, especially big ones, will gather at river mouths to feed on

salmon entering the river to spawn and on dead carcasses of the spawned out fish as they are washed downstream. Fish the

shallow water right in the river mouth at high tide, and the bottom of the alluvial fan (where silt from the river builds up a shelf) at low tide.

4. **.Back Eddies** - Plankton, krill, and other tiny organisms are the primary food source of herring and other bait fish. They

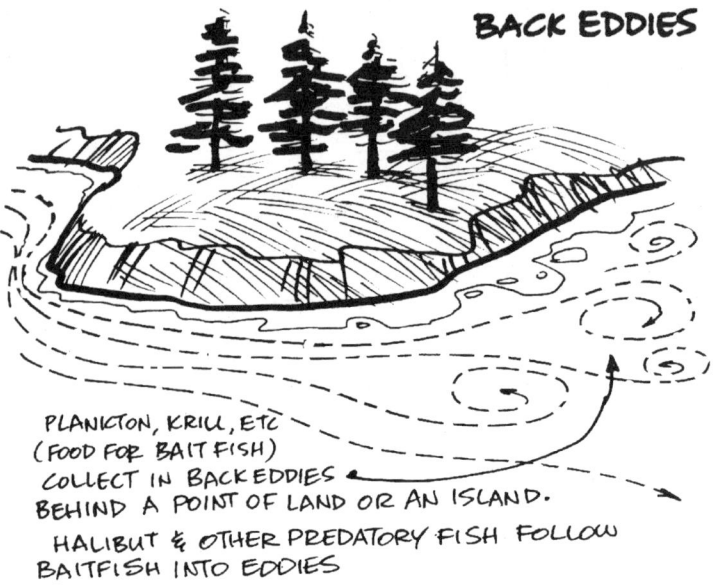

BACK EDDIES

PLANKTON, KRILL, ETC (FOOD FOR BAIT FISH) COLLECT IN BACK EDDIES BEHIND A POINT OF LAND OR AN ISLAND. HALIBUT & OTHER PREDATORY FISH FOLLOW BAITFISH INTO EDDIES

have little power of locomotion and are swept into quiet back eddies where the bait fish will gather to feed. The larger predatory fish - salmon, rockfish, lingcod, mackerel, and halibut, follow the baitfish into these eddies to feed on them.

Back eddies are formed when the tide or current moves past a point of land and the water circles around behind it, forming a pool of quieter water. This is also where the floating weed and debris will gather, so you will have to deal with cleaning your line periodically.

5. **Vertical Eddies** - This is where a change in depth, especially an abrupt change, lying across a tidal flow, causes the water to change direction and create a vertical "pocket" where bait fish will gather. You will often see these vertical eddies as "boils" of turbulent water near a shallow reef.

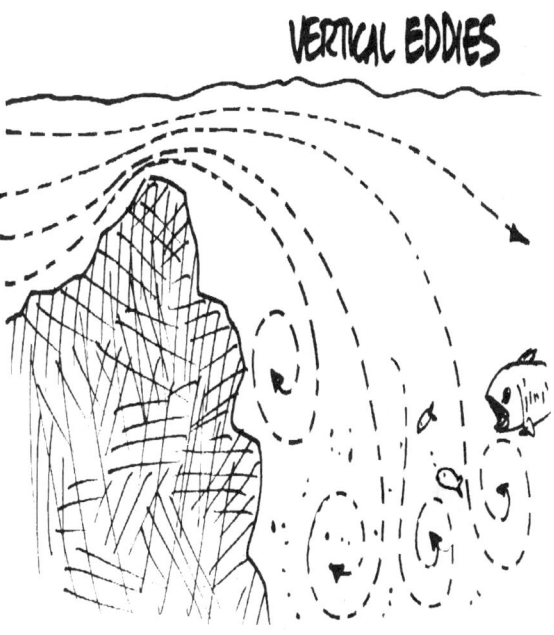

6. **Tide lines** - Opposing currents in open water (sometimes part of a giant back-eddy many miles across) will trap plankton and krill, as well as baitfish. Hungry gamefish prowl these tidelines. When working with our underwater camera, we often see concentrations of salmon and other fish as we pass across tidelines.

7. **Feeding seabirds** - Seagulls are like aerial spotter planes that can see concentrations of bait not visible from a boat on the surface. These gulls are great for locating shallow feeding salmon, but not so important for halibut

Diving birds, often erroneously called diving "ducks", can locate baitfish to depths of 100 feet or more. They can be a mildly encouraging sign for halibut, but certainly not a primary clue to finding them.

8.   Probably the most important and practical way to find halibut is to ask questions. Ask the tackle store manager where you buy your gear or bait. He is usually eager to help. If you are successful, you will buy more tackle, and bring your friends.

Ask other anglers at the marina or boat launch ramp. Go there in the afternoon or when the wind comes up and the boats are coming home from their day's outing. If you see someone with halibut, ask them where, when, and how. Location, depth and lure choice are the most important questions. Some anglers are quite secretive about their methods, but others are proud of their success and willing to share information with others.

I get really excited when I see a good catch, and approach the angler with positive enthusiasm and curiosity. After congratulating him or her and admiring the catch, I ask exactly where they were caught, how deep, and with what lure. Sometimes I get a vacant stare and a mumble about "got them out there", but usually I get some <u>very</u> valuable tips. If they are very cooperative, I might ask for more details on when was the "bite" time, use of scent, or bait rigging details.

Another good way to learn is to go out on the water in the general area where halibut are being taken. Get out at the first crack of daylight and watch the other boats. Get in among them, fish the same drifts, over the same bottom, and keep your lure or bait right on the bottom. If other boats are catching fish, you know you have solved the biggest problem, finding the right spot.

Now just keep observing, with binoculars if possible, how fast they are drifting. You can also ask questions as you drift near other boats. Keep making adjustments, imitating the successful boats, and soon you'll have the thrill of a fish of you own!

Chapter Six
Lures and Baits

When I first started fishing halibut, I was told they were indiscriminate feeders who would bite on anything. "Get any bait or lure close to them, and they'll grab it," I was advised by a supposed halibut expert. While I had my suspicions about this information, I tried fishing this way, putting down baits and lures without much concern for details, concentrating instead on finding the proper locations.

I had no luck, and thought this was OK, since no one else was catching any. Then I watched Tim Harrison from Harrison Cove Lodge in Barkley Sound take three nice halibut while everyone else was skunked. Catching one fish, even two, might be luck, but three in a row, while 20 other boats got nothing, convinced me that technique, bait and lure presentation was very important indeed.

Talking with Tim and others, and extensive study with our underwater cameras, has taught me how to increase the odds for catching halibut. First consideration, of course, is to be at the right spot at the right time. Then the fine details of lure and/or bait and how to work it across the halibut beds determine who gets the fish.

Natural Bait

Hungry halibut will take many natural baits, and this is where my original advice (They'll take anything!) comes closest to the truth. Herring, anchovies, salmon heads, salmon bellies, whole cod or pollock, cod bellies, squid, and octopus are all successful natural baits. Add extra scent and they all work better. (More on scent later on.)

As with any sport fishing technique, matching the natural food in the area is important. "Matching the hatch" is the byword of the fly fishermen, and this holds true for all species. Ideally, you should examine the stomach contents of a fresh caught halibut to see what they are eating today. Failing that, you can ask other boats, or keep changing baits until you find one that works.

But halibut will usually take a variety of baits on any given day.

Herring, octopus, or squid are favorites with halibut, and they will

59

often take these baits no matter what the natural feed at the time. Salmon heads, salmon bellies, cod bellies seem to be more successful when the halibut are feeding on these varieties. This is especially true near river mouths when big halibut are feeding on spawning salmon.

Hook the bait on your single or tandem rig as shown in the illustrations, add some scent, then drop to the bottom and bounce gently along, pulling rod tip up and down about 18 inches to two feet when fishing at depths under 100 feet using nylon monofilament and weights of six ounces or less. As you go deeper, or use heavier weight, you'll need to pull the rod in a greater arc to get the desired action.

Our underwater camera showed that halibut, (or any fish, including salmon) do not like a lure which oscillates more than about two feet, especially if jerked vigorously. It is too hard to catch and they give up quickly. The goal is to have a short pull, followed by a slack rod drop of a foot or less.

If you are drifting off the side of a hump, or on a sloping bottom, peel off a bit of line every few jigs, to

make sure the lure touches bottom regularly.

Artificial Lures

The same basic rules apply to artificials as to bait, except that proper action is even more important. You can get strikes on natural bait which is hanging motionless, but artificials <u>must</u> be kept in motion. A fish biting an artificial will spit it out very quickly, as we learned from watching our underwater footage. If the lure is moving, a sticky sharp hook is much more likely to strike home. A motionless artificial hardly ever triggers a strike. Fish will approach and turn away at the last moment. In my opinion, their eyes are sharp enough that they can see that the motionless lure is artificial, as opposed to the texture and appearance of the real thing.

As with bait, short pulls are important so the fish can catch the lure more easily. Because of the stretch of monofilament, I think non-stretch line is more important for artificials than for bait, especially at more than 100 feet in depth or in tides and wind. Braided dacron can be used if cost is a factor, but the much thinner diameter Spectra or Spiderwire are better choices for most conditions.

Bouncing the jig on the bottom not only assures that you are, in fact, on the bottom; it also can create a disturbance that will attract fish. Sound waves from a thud on the bottom will travel a long way to attract a fish from well beyond the sight range. Using a spinner on your jig will also send out a fluttering vibration like a wounded baitfish. (We've developed some jigs with spinners. See order section.) Bouncing a jig on fine sand bottom can also send up a puff of sand to attract fish within sight of the lure.

Combination Bait and Artificial
Sometimes a combination bait/artificial rig will work better than either one individually. We find that a piece of bait—herring, squid, octopus — added to the tail of any jig will increase its effectiveness for any fish. We use this combination all the time when fishing for sole, flounder, and cod near my home north of Victoria in British Columbia.
Adding bait to leadhead jigs with hootchie or flutter tails will also increase their effectiveness in most instances.

Some anglers decorate their bait rigs with artificials to add more fish catching power. Sliding a hootchie on top of a herring gives it an added wiggle, and some extra color.

Using Scent

I always thought that the natural scent given off by a bait was enough to attract fish, but I changed my mind after conversations with teachers and professors at the prestigious School of Fisheries at the University of Washington at Seattle.

I do guest lectures there several times a year, and show them underwater video on my experiments on fish behavior. (One test showed that salmon would strike a lure soaked in my oily bilge in preference to a clean lure.) Their research people were very interested and told me of their tests using various aromatic hydrocarbons and amino acids to attract feeding fish, some of which would be contained in my bilgewater!

Using information on fish attractants, we developed a product called Formula X-10 Fish Feeding Stimulant. Our tests over the past four years have proven to me beyond the shadow of a doubt that adding scent to a lure can increase your catch by two, three fold or more. We put two identical lures side by side behind our underwater camera and watched the fish chose the scented lure more than three to one. We got similar results fishing identical lures on both sides of the boat, one with X-10 and one without.

Most of our tests have been on salmon, with quite a few on sole and flatfish, and limited tests on halibut (because we have such a tough time finding them with our underwater camera!). However, we are getting lots of enthusiastic feedback from customers who use Formula X-10 in Washington, British Columbia, and Alaska.

Ian Langejan, part owner of a tackle distribution company in Victoria, reports that he was having no luck jigging for halibut in Juan de Fuca until he added X-10 and caught a 92 pound barn door, the largest fish by far of any taken that day. Many similar stories have the same theme - X-10 catches the most and the biggest! (Pardon my enthusiastic endorsement, but I'm very convinced of its value and importance in improving your catch.)

How much scent should you use? The more the better! A strong scent plume can attract fish from quite a distance.

I am a firm believer in appealing to more than one of the fish's senses. Many lures have only visual appeal, using size, color, shape, and action, all visual stimuli. Adding a spinner will appeal to the sense of hearing or vibration. Scent adds another sense to give the fish another reason to strike. It's like passing the chocolate shop or an outdoor barbeque. Those heavenly aromas put you in the mood for food!

I think that most strike decisions are made from sight stimulus,

but adding vibration and scent gives the fish more evidence that your lure is something worth eating. These other senses also help attract fish from beyond the sight range. With North Pacific underwater visibility usually in the 15 to 50 foot range, it's vital

65

to bring the fish close enough to see the bait. Scent and vibration can cause fish to "home in" on your lure from hundreds of feet away, long before they can see it!

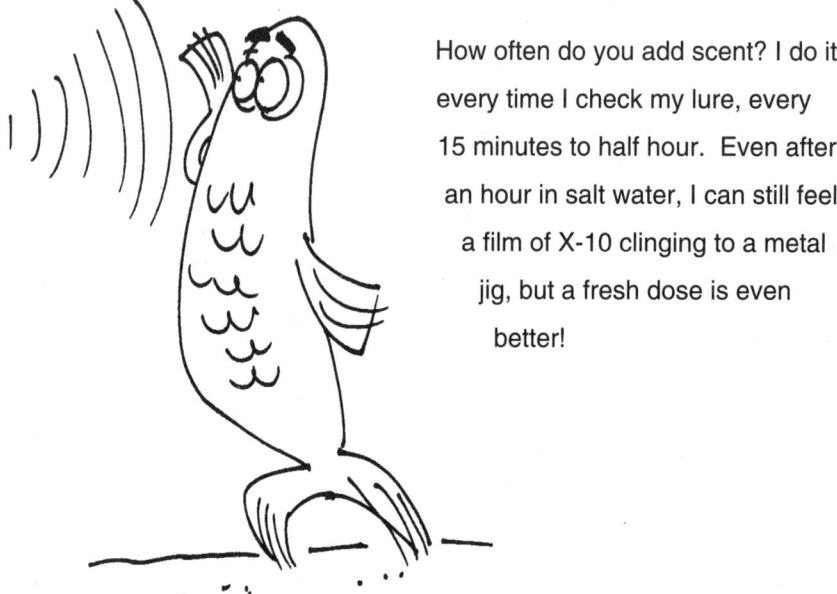

How often do you add scent? I do it every time I check my lure, every 15 minutes to half hour. Even after an hour in salt water, I can still feel a film of X-10 clinging to a metal jig, but a fresh dose is even better!

Chapter Seven

Lure Presentation

Since halibut live right on the bottom, all lure and bait presentations should concentrate on keeping your offering as close as possible to the bottom.

Drifting with a slow moving tide on a flat or gradually deepening bottom will give the fish a good long look at your lure as it passes by. Keep the lure moving, up slowly, then a quicker drop to the bottom. Pause a few seconds after the bait hits bottom before repeating. Big halibut will often grab a bait, or even a jig, when it hesitates between jigging strokes.

When the tide is moving more quickly, you'll need more weight to stay on the bottom. Better still,

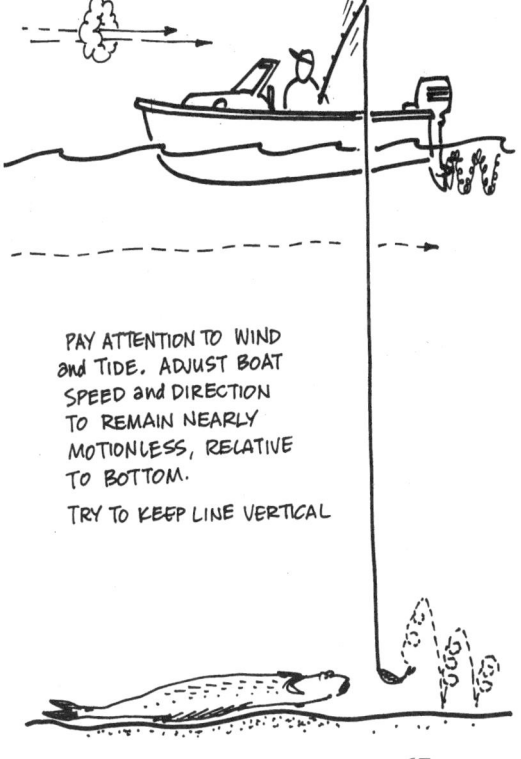

PAY ATTENTION TO WIND and TIDE. ADJUST BOAT SPEED and DIRECTION TO REMAIN NEARLY MOTIONLESS, RELATIVE TO BOTTOM.

TRY TO KEEP LINE VERTICAL

67

run your trolling motor slowly against the tide to give a slower bottom drift. When the wind is blowing, motoring against it will accomplish the same thing. You can also use a sea-anchor, but wind and tide have to be exactly right to allow this to work. Using your motor is better.

When the bottom is dead flat, with no outcroppings, you can rig your bait or lure to give a wounded fish action, with lots of scent, and just let it drift with the rod in the holder. Keep a close eye on the sounder for depth changes, and lower the rod tip periodically to be sure you are still on the bottom.

Downriggers are also very effective in this situation. You can lower the seven- to ten-pound weight until it hits bottom, crank up a foot or two, and let it drift along. If you get a strike using this method, you'll also be able to play your halibut with no weight on the line after it trips free.

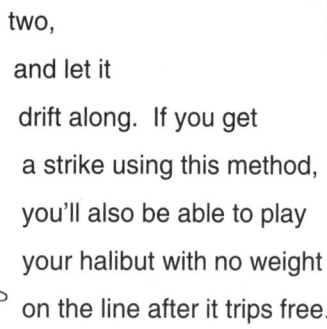

Another advantage of downrigger fishing is the opportunity to add an attracting flasher on a short line attached to the downrigger weight. When using our underwater camera, we add such a flasher under the camera when we are trolling, and just above the cameras when we are jigging. It seems to attract more fish of all species into the vicinity, both from the reflective flash and from the vibrating thump of the attractor.

Is there a "best" lure or bait?

When giving seminars around the country, from Alaska to San Diego, from New York to Seattle, I always get the same question when I complete my presentation on baits and lures for salmon, or any other fish.

"What is the 'best' lure?" they ask plaintively. "With all your experience and research observations, you must have come up with one lure that beats all the rest!" "It depends on the conditions," is my reply, "and the natural feed in the water at the time." This is especially true for salmon, which can be feeding on herring, anchovies, squid, shrimp, or needlefish. Each requires a different lure and presentation method.

For halibut, the choice is a bit easier. Although they feed on mid-water swimmers like herring, squid or even salmon, they are primarily bottom feeders and spend most of their lives there. Predominant food items living on the bottom include shrimp, crab, and octopus, and stomach content analysis by the International Halibut Commission confirms that these *are* the predominant foods of young halibut. All of these creatures are brown to reddish orange in color and all have legs or protruding appendages.

If you used a large, reddish-brown, hootchie-octopus rig and jigged it to keep the tentacles moving, you would closely imitate a small octopus and have a reasonable facsimile of a crab or large shrimp. I think a halibut probably prefers small octopus, since they are all meat — no claws, pincers, or spiky nose to make them hard to chew or swallow. (This is just a speculation on my part - but it makes good sense.)

Stomach contents of larger halibut contain a much larger percentage of fish - cod, pollock, and sole - but my hunch is that they would still prefer an octopus if it was easy pickings. The major exception is fishing at river mouths when halibut are gorging on salmon. Salmon heads or bellies should be used at that time.

Last, and not least, be sure to add lots of scent to the lure. That Formula X-10 aroma brings them in and puts them in a feeding mood.

Chapter Eight

How They Bite

There are lots of theories on how halibut actually take a bait or lure. Some insist they are random feeders that will bite on anything that they can see. Others feel that they are more discerning, and advocate a particular bait or lure as the best under any circumstances. Some claim that halibut actually "sit" on the bait, covering it with their large, flat body to immobilize it before striking. They support this theory by pointing out that many halibut are foul hooked, and this is caused by their "sitting" behavior.

I've watched on the underwater camera over 100 halibut approach our lures and baits, and none have tried to cover or smother the bait. Many approach and turn away at the last split second, their bodies brushing against the lure as they turn. If your jig moves upward at that moment, it can snag against the side of the body, and hook the fish in the side. We have actually watched this happen on at least two occasions.

As the fish got within an inch or two of the lure, there was a very sudden and strong sucking action. The lure disappeared into the halibut's mouth so fast we could barely see it go -- even with stop-frame video analysis. The bait would move completely inside the mouth in one video frame -- 1/30 0f a second!

Chapter Nine

Playing and Landing Halibut

Once you have hooked any halibut over about 15 pounds, you are in for an exciting ride, especially for the first few minutes. Halibut typically inhale the lure, shake their head vigorously (we've watched them toss a two pound weight like a rag doll), then streak away in a screaming run that can peel hundreds of feet off the reel in less than 90 seconds.

This is one of the two most critical moments in playing any gamefish, who most always run

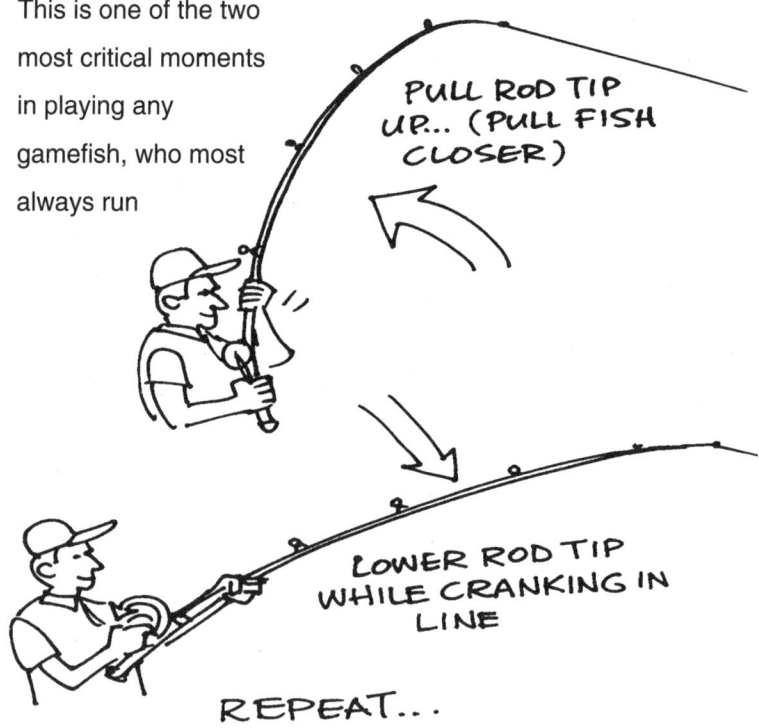

powerfully away when they feel the tug of the hook in their jaw. If you are using a slipping clutch reel, you must pre-set the clutch tension <u>before</u> you put the line out, to a pressure which allows a smooth run-out against a resistance of your choosing.

If you try to adjust the tension during that first frantic run, you risk setting it too tight and breaking off the fish, or too loose, and having a horrendous backlash tangle, which will also probably cost you the fish.

If using a single action "knuckle duster" reel, set a basic medium tension on the drag screw, then use your skill to palm the reel to apply the necessary extra drag to control the fish. This is the most exciting and skill testing way to play a halibut, and I'm comfortable with it for fish up to 75 or even 100 pounds. Above that size, I'd rather have a geared reel to get the leverage to keep up the necessary pressure.

(I've developed a sport fish simulator device to give anglers practice in handling a running fish. It consists of a black box into which runs the line from your reel. A videotape in your VCR shows an underwater picture on the TV as the fish strikes, and a signal to the black box activates the line. As the fish rushes away on the TV screen, the line

screams off your reel, and you play your fish in a very realistic manner. It provides good practice and lots of fun with both single action and geared reels.)

After the first run, the fish will usually stop to shake his head to dislodge the hook, then take off again, often in a different direction. This "different direction" can be straight back toward the boat! Be ready to crank as fast as you can to keep tension on the line, and pull back hard on the rod to help maintain that tension.

There may be yet another run, but many fish just settle down on

the bottom at this point. This "sulking" behavior can be frustrating. You want to keep the fish moving to tire him out, but there is only so much pressure you can exert on a heavy fish. Here are three maneuvers which can help get the fish moving again:

1. "Strum" the line. I've used this technique many times to move a heavy fish off the bottom - big Chinook salmon, lingcod, and halibut. Simply "plunk" the taut line near the reel, just like playing a guitar or banjo, but with more force. This will send a strong vibration right down to the lure, often

   irritating the fish into swimming away.

2. Bang the rod butt -- with the palm of your hand, or thump it against the gunwale of the boat. This also sends a shock wave down to the lure.

3. Move the boat - Pulling straight up on a bottom hugging fish seems to encourage it to keep pulling down to stay on the bottom. If you move the boat off to the side about 100 to 300 feet, it changes the angle considerably and the fish moves more easily, often swimming off in another strong run.

Playing halibut, especially a big one, usually settles down to a tug of war, with the angler pulling the largely played out fish through the resistance of the water. Keep pulling at an angle, so you use the flat shape to your advantage as an upwardly planing surface to "sail" the fish toward the surface. When the fish is near or at the surface, move the boat close to the fish and prepare for the second critical moment in playing a fish.

More gamefish are lost right at the boat than at any time after the first frantic run after the strike. Several important precautions apply:

1. Don't lift the head or body of the fish out of the water. The exhausted fish is often quite docile beside the boat, but raising the head deprives the gills of oxygen, and the alarmed fish makes one last dash for freedom, tearing the

hooks or breaking the gear before the angler can react.

2. For a fish under 40 or 50 pounds, you can use a net, but be sure to net the fish head first. A tail first attempt gives the fish a powerful lever. He flexes his powerful tail against the net and shoots out like a diver off a board. When you net head first, the fish swims forward, deeper into the net - where you want it. Be sure to hold the net vertical when lifting.

3. Using a Gaff - For halibut under 50 pounds, a gaff is also a viable option, but only if you really know how to handle a gaff. Plunging a gaff into a powerful halibut (they are just one huge muscle!), ties you rigidly to a bucking bronco, twisting and turning the gaff and often wrenching it loose. I've watched big salmon, ling and

halibut swim away with a gaff sticking straight up, like the periscope of a submarine.

I like a gaff with a hooked end. it will hold better than a straight spike, which is OK for salmon which can be scooped right into the boat. You will almost certainly have a "wrestling match" with the halibut and the more closed "hook" shape will hold better.

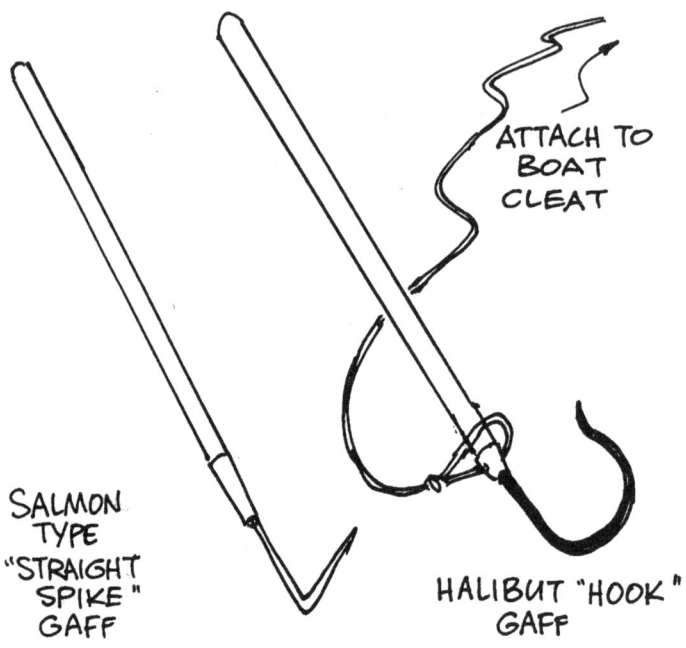

A "flying" gaff, where the head of the gaff pulls loose from the handle, is an excellent tool for handling small to medium halibut. A strong line tied to the head of the gaff and anchored on a boat cleat gives the fish room to thrash around and tire himself.

4.	Harpoon - This is my favorite method for handling a medium to heavyweight barn door. A harpoon is a spear shaped device with a releasing head which is plunged into the fish, and a locking clip which holds the head in the fish. Harpoons are more accurate, have more penetrating power, and are easier to use than a gaff. As with a flying gaff, the harpoon head is tied to the boat so the fish can pull against the boat until he is exhausted.

The best place to impale a harpoon is in the shoulder, just behind the gill cover and near the lateral line. You can spear him through the head and maybe even kill him at the same time,

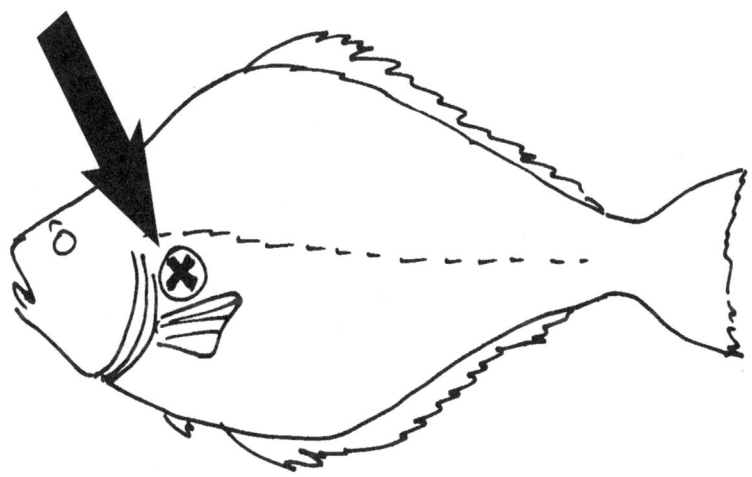

but the skull area is much harder, and the gaff can slip off to the side, and not impale the fish, which will thrash violently and may get off the line.

5. Shooting or Clubbing the Fish - A large, stubborn fish can be completely subdued with a well placed pistol shot to the brain. However, this can be quite a problem. In many areas, including here in British Columbia, using a firearm in this manner is completely illegal! Even where legal, it is a difficult and potentially dangerous practice. The halibut's brain is tiny in relation to its overall size, and is a small and erratically moving target.

Some old time halibut veterans shoot their fish regularly and successfully, but I recommend against it. I also think that trying to club a fish has a poor chance of success. It is very difficult to hit exactly the right spot, and easy to hit the line in error and knock the lure loose.

Small Boat Warning

On a cruise to Alaska in 1974, I walked around a small boat harbor, admiring the huge dungeness crabs caught by a local teenager. As I started down the long ramp to the dock, I was startled to see a large sign warning sport anglers not to bring large halibut on board small boats. There had been three fatalities that year when powerful halibut had smashed the floorboards of wooden boats, capsizing the boats and drowning the occupants.

I also learned about broken legs and arms inflicted when fishermen tried to subdue a halibut thrashing wildly in the cockpit of a boat. Large halibuts' muscle power is awesome, and care should be taken to protect yourself.

I like to subdue large fish <u>outside</u> the boat. After harpooning the fish, I let him swim around for a few minutes (when he sometimes tows the boat a hundred feet or more) then bring him to the side of the boat. When he is quite docile, we slip a loop over the tail and cinch it down. Then we loop it around the rope to the harpoon and pull tight until the fish is bent into a "C" shape. Then we just leave him tied to the side of the boat until he expires.

Chapter Ten

Care and Cleaning of the Catch

Many successful anglers bleed their catch, which is a good idea for any fish, to improve its table quality. Tear out a piece of gill tissue, or stick a sharp knife into the soft flesh at the bottom of the gill cover while the fish is still alive or immediately after clubbing it to death. The resulting blood flow can cause a big mess in your fish box or cockpit, but the clean white fillets you get can make it worthwhile. If possible, tear out some gill rakers while the fish is still in the water and your boat remains clean.

Put the fish in a fish box or insulated cooler as soon as he is bled. If you add ice or plastic ice packs, so much the better. Hanging the fish in the water is better than leaving it lying on the dock, but surface water temperatures can reach 55 to 60 degrees Fahrenheit and fish quality will suffer if left for long periods.

I keep burlap bags on board for gathering clams and oysters. If you dip these bags (or towels) into the water and spread them over the carcass, the evaporation cooling will be of great benefit. Moisten the bags every 15 minutes to half hour to maintain the cooling effect.

While it is impractical on many small boats, removing the gills and entrails right away is another big step toward tasty fillets. I do this with my salmon, rock fish, and ling cod, and the results are noticeably better than fish left in the round until the end of the day.

Filleting a big halibut for the first time is an experience long remembered. I helped clean and fillet a 150 pound monster caught at Nimmo Bay Lodge on the central British Columbia coast. Owner Craig Murray had long, sharp carving knives and a big stainless steel table ready, and we literally climbed up on the carcass to place the knife for some of the cuts. It seemed less like a fish and more like butchering a steer or pig.

Chapter Eleven

A Gourmet Treat!

Halibut is considered by many to be the finest eating fish in the sea. Even those who rate other fish higher, put halibut very near the top of the list. Frozen halibut is very good if properly frozen, but eating it fresh is always better.

I fish for halibut only a few times a year, and it is tempting to put a cache in the freezer for the in between months. While I still put down a few fillets, I like to share the fresh fish, and its wonderful flavor and texture, with family, friends, and neighbors.

When I got that 121-pounder off Sidney a few years ago, all the relatives and the neighbors for a quarter mile on each side of our property, got a couple of pounds of fresh fillets! I loved seeing the joy on their faces when they picked it up. I still get friendly greetings from them and a frequent question, "How's the fishing?"

My wife Darlene has compiled all our favorite recipes into a new seafood cookbook. Write for more details. Meanwhile, here are a few tasty halibut recipes.

Darlene's Halibut Recipes.

Halibut Ceviche
(aka Seviche) - a wonderful warm weather appetizer.

Ceviche is a unique method of "cooking" fish by marinating it in lime and/or lemon juice. Charlie and I were first introduced to Ceviche in Mexico years ago. Since then we've tried many variations. Most call for jalapeno or other hot peppers, in true Mexican fashion. Try this one "hot", or "cool" -- as presented here. Either way, it's delicious. Special thanks to Kevin White and John Robbins. Recipe serves four to six..

1 lb halibut cut in 1/2" cubes
Juice of 2 large fresh limes.

Marinate together in covered glass bowl for 3 hours, stirring occasionally. When "cooked", fish will be white.

1/2 lb vine ripened tomatoes (peeled and seeded)
1/4 sweet green pepper (or jalapeno)
1/2 cup finely chopped fresh cilantro (or parsley)
2 tbsp red wine vinegar
1/4 cup olive oil
Dash of tabasco
1/2 tsp dried oregano
Salt and pepper to taste

Dice tomatoes and peppers and add to Ceviche, along with olive oil, vinegar, tabasco, salt and pepper. Refrigerate. To add some Mexican "heat" to the Ceviche, add 1/2 to 1 tsp red pepper flakes.

1 small avocado, peeled and diced
6 to 10 sliced stuffed green(or black) olives

Serve Ceviche in a large sea shell, or seafood cocktail glass. Garnish with the last 2 items. If there must be a delay between peeling and serving, you can prevent the avocado from darkening by sprinkling it with lemon or lime juice and covering it.

Barbecued Seafood Kebabs

Visitors to the Pacific Northwest enjoy our laid-back life style. As much as barbecued beef in Alberta or pitchfork steaks in Saskatchewan, this recipe typifies us. Marinate the seafood before your guests arrive, and thread the bamboo skewers just before cooking. Serves six as a main course, more as an hors d'ouvre.

2 lb halibut
2 lb salmon; **Cut salmon and halibut in 1 inch cubes, remove bones and skin.**
24 prawns, shelled and de-veined
24 mussels, shelled and washed.

Marinade:
2 cups fresh orange juice
1 tbsp grated orange rind
1 cup olive oil
1/2 cup liquid honey
1 tbsp crushed black peppercorns
Salt to taste
2 to 3 dozen wooden skewers

Mix marinade and pour over sea food. Cover and refrigerate 6 hours.
Soak skewers for at least an hour so they don't burn

Thread seafood on skewers alternately. Cook them on a hot oiled grill or barbecue for about ten minutes, brushing frequently with marinade. As barbecue heats vary wildly, watch the halibut - when it is just white throughout, whether it's three minutes, or 15, it's done.

Golden Deep Fried Halibut

Try this coating on cod and other whitefish, as well. We tried it on Moi (the fish only Hawaiian royalty was once allowed to eat) in Kauai and found it delicious. Serves six to eight.

2 lb fresh halibut **Remove bones and skin and cut in portion sized pieces**
3 cups fine bread crumbs
1 tsp garlic powder
1/4 tsp cayenne pepper
2 tbsp finely chopped fresh parsley
1 tsp salt

Mix well together
1-2 cups flour
3 eggs, beaten with 1/2 cup water

Coat fish well with flour. Dip in egg mixture, then coat with crumb mixture. Deep fry in vegetable oil at 350° for 3 or 4 minutes, or until just done - watch carefully. Or pan fry for 3 to 4 minutes.

Clay Baked Halibut in Parchment

No matter how beautifully you freeze it, families of frequent fishers know the difference between fresh caught seafood and frozen. We have found baking seafood in a covering - seaweed, banana leaves, grape leaves, you name it - to be the answer to retaining moisture and winning compliments. This is a very "today" recipe - move over, Martha Stewart. Serves six to eight.

2 lb halibut, skin and bones removed
Cut in 2 -1/2 " to 3" squares

Compote:

4 Grapefruit sections
1/4 cup minced cilantro leaves
1 jalapeno chili pepper, seeded, deveined, and minced
1 clove garlic, minced
1 tablespoon fresh lime juice
2 teaspoons olive oil

6 to 8 pieces of 10" X 10" parchment
6 to 8 pieces of colored raffia
Clay baker and lid, soaked for 1/2 hour before using

Place halibut pieces on parchment and top each with a large spoonful of compote. Wrap carefully and tie with raffia. Make one extra piece for a tester. Arrange in clay baker, cover with lid and place in cold oven. Turn heat to 350°. Cook for 30 minutes. Check the tester for doneness. Serve immediately. Expect raves.

Note: If you use a regular baking dish instead of a clay baker, heat the oven to 350° and cook for no more than 10 min before testing, as the clay baker takes much longer.

We are involved in many fishing-related projects. We would be pleased to send you information on any of the following:

- **FISHING LODGES**
Many of the top fishing resorts and lodges -- from the Arctic, Alaska, British Columbia, Mexico, Costa Rica, and other areas -- support our research by hosting our field research team while we get our underwater pictures.
Please let us know where you would like to go and we will send you complete details!

- **The "SPORTFISHIN' SIMULATOR"**
This very realistic fishing experience uses an ingenious computer-activated device to create the heart-pumping thrill of a big salmon, sailfish, bass, or trout tearing line from your reel while you watch the underwater action on your television screen! It also keeps score so you can measure your improvement or compete with your friends.
It's ideal for resorts, sports bars, fund-raising events.

- **FORMULA X-10 FISH FEEDING STIMULANT**
Developed in conjunction with a University Professor, Formula X-10 triggers most gamefish to strike. It adds that extra temptation that turns a hesitant fish into an aggressive feeder!. Four years of research show X-10 outfished untreated lures by more than three to one! Research-tested on salmon, halibut, trout, sturgeon, steelhead, and other species.
55 ml   -- $4.50 each   --   3 / $10.00

- **PICTURE-PERFECT LURE**
Watching slow-motion replays of salmon strikes, Charlie noticed that fishes' eyes "scanned" the lure -- almost like a dollar-bill change machine. When our lure matched the picture in the fish's computer brain, they engulfed the lure!
Laminating a four-color reflective herring photo on a jointed-action body, the Picture Perfect Lure combines erratic swimming motion with sonic vibration and image accuracy to trigger strikes on all salt-water game fish!
$5.99 ea or 3 / $10.00

- **HOOKSHARP**
One of Charlie's most important discoveries was that fish are striking at our lures more often than we dream -- but dull hooks bounce right out of their mouths! Even brand new hooks are not sharp enough, and all hooks need touching up daily. Hooksharp makes it quick and easy to keep a "sticky-sharp" point on your hooks. If it won't stick easily to your fingernail, it won't stick in the hard, bony mouth of a salmon or halibut!

Mail Order Special   -- $19.95

VIDEOS

Charlie White TV Episodes on Video — The Ideal Gift

Video #1 — FAREWELL HARBOUR HALIBUT
Get the first ever look at how these deep feeding monsters react to baits and lures.
$19.95

Video #2 — COLUMBIA RIVER WALLEYE
Canada's most popular freshwater gamefish. See the amazing discovery of how a unique lure presentation stimulated immediate strikes.
$19.95

Video #3 — STURGEON
Now see some awesome underwater sequences of Sturgeon feeding behaviour.
$19.95

Video #4 — LURE RESEARCH AT HAKAI PASS
Killer whales share the spotlight with jumping Coho. The underwater camera reveals how fish use their computer-like brains to choose which lure to strike.
$19.95

Video #5 — TOFINO CHINOOK
An exciting West Coast adventure, fishing for the largest of the five species of Pacific Salmon. Watch 30 to 55 lb. salmon strikes.
$19.95

Video #6 — MILLIONS OF PINK SALMON
In crystal clear water these plankton feeders choose small plastic "hootchies". Includes best trolling speed, how scents work, getting proper lure action.
$19.95

Video #7 — LIGHT AND COLOUR
Are fish colour blind? We watch salmon making colour choices when confronted by side-by-side lures. We see how water refraction changes colour as we go deeper, and how baitfish change colour to match our surroundings.
$19.95

Video #8 — CAMPBELL RIVER LIVE HERRING
Is live Herring the ultimate fishing lure? Our cameras watch salmon, lingcod, Pacific sharks, and rock fish react to our live herring.
$19.95

Video #9 — SOLE & FLATFISH
Fascinating underwater footage of life on the bottom in a quiet bay near Victoria, B.C. A young family catches sole, sanddabs, even a baby octopus!
$19.95

Video #10 — JIGGING FOR SALMON
New designs use vibrations and sound waves to attract fish. Our spellbinding underwater footage shows jigging techniques most likely to trigger strikes.
$19.95

Video #11 — WINTER CHINOOK
Great sport and tasty eating. Predatory seals attack our hooked salmon followed by an exciting tug of war!
$19.95

Video #12 — COSTA RICA TARPON
First ever underwater strike footage of tarpon, plus explosive action and slow motion jumps. Underwater footage of a big school of Jack Crevalle.
$19.95

Video #13 — COSTA RICA SAILFISH
Spectacular underwater strikes and dramatic slow motion jumps highlight this tropical adventure. Curious Porpoises investigate the underwater camera. Large Dorado hide out under floating logs.
$19.95

Video #14 — WHITEHORSE CHAR & RAINBOW
Charlie's research crew travels to Whitehorse in the Yukon Territories for ice fishing. At a frozen lake cameras are lowered under the ice to show winter trout behaviour, seeing beautiful ice patterns from below.
$19.95

WHY FISH STRIKE, WHY THEY DON'T Feature length adventure using underwater cameras to see how salmon strike, and how they react to different lures, spoons, plugs, flies, & natural bait. 88 min. Code # WFS $24.95 	**SAVE! When you buy more than one of the above 30 min. videos!** 1 video = $19.95 each 2 - 4 videos = $17.95 each 5 - 8 videos = $15.95 each 9 or more videos = $13.95 each **SAVE! When you buy both of our feature length videos for just $39.90** **SAVE EVEN MORE!** When you buy the entire Charlie White 16 Video Library! for just: $199.00	**IN SEARCH OF THE ULTIMATE LURE** Join Charlie and guest comedian Arte Johnson to see how many species strike — Salmon, Trout, Steelhead, Pike, Marlin, Barracuda, & more. Incredible footage of killer whales attacking sea lions. 88 min. Code #SUL $24.95 

YOU CAN GET CHARLIE WHITE'S FISHING PRODUCTS BY MAIL ORDER!

SEND ORDER FORM TO:
SALTAIRE PUBLISHING
P.O. Box 2003
Sidney, B.C., CANADA
V8L 3S3
Phone (250) 655-3573   Fax (250) 655-3573

ORDERED BY

SHIP TO   PHONE

CITY   FAX:

PROV/STATE   PC / ZIP

DATE

ITEM #	QNTY	COLOR	DESCRIPTION	ITEM	QNTY	TOTAL

MERCHANDISE TOTAL

PRICES SUBJECT TO CHANGE WITHOUT NOTICE

PST (BC) ONLY 7% Merchandise

SHIPPING & HANDLING

GST (Canada only) 7% Merchandise + S&H

TOTAL

SEND CHEQUE OR MONEY ORDER ONLY

SHIPPING & HANDLING:
- •$4.00 for 1st Video / $1.00 for each additional Video
- •$4.00 for 1st $10.00 value of other merchandise / $1.00 for each additional $10.00 of merchandise